The Caravan

Diary of S. N. Goenka's "Meditation Now" Tour
Europe and North America
April 10 to August 15, 2002

Vipassana Research Institute
Dhamma Giri, Igatpuri 422 403, India

© 2004 by Vipassana Research Institute
All rights reserved

First Edition: 2004

ISBN 81-7414-254-1

Price : Rs. 80/-

Published by:
Vipassana Research Institute
Dhamma Giri, Igatpuri 422 403
Dist. Nashik, Maharashtra, India
Tel: [91] (2553) 244076, 244086
Fax: [91] (2553) 244176
E-mail: info@giri.dhamma.org
Website: www.vri.dhamma.org

Yattha kho, āvuso, na jāyati na jīyati na mīyati na cavati na upapajjati, nāhaṃ taṃ gamanena lokassa antaṃ ñāteyyaṃ daṭṭheyyaṃ patteyyanti vadāmī"ti...

Na kho panāhaṃ, āvuso, appatvā lokassa antaṃ dukkhassa antakiriyaṃ vadāmi.

Api ca khvāhaṃ, āvuso, imasmiṃyeva byāmamatte kaḷevare sasaññimhi samanake lokañca paññapemi lokasamudayañca lokanirodhañca lokanirodhagāminiñca paṭipadanti.

Friend, I say that the end of the world where one is not born, does not age, does not die, does not pass away, and is not reborn, cannot be known, seen or reached by travelling to the end of the world.

However, friend, I say that without having reached the end of the world, there is no end to suffering.

It is, friend, in this fathom-long body with its perception and mind that I make known the world, the origin of the world, the cessation of the world and the way leading to the cessation of the world.

Saṃyutta Nikāya 1.1.107, Rohitassa Sutta

Preface

In 2002, at the age of 78, Goenkaji embarked on a remarkable Dhamma tour of the West. He traveled for 128 days through Europe and North America, giving many Dhamma talks, leading meditation sessions, giving media interviews and guiding students in private interviews along the way. The United Kingdom was the first stop of Goenkaji's tour. He arrived in London on April 10 and left on April 18 for New York.

There, he began the second leg of the journey of over 13,000 miles of road through the United States and Canada to spread the gift of Dhamma with compassion and joy.

He returned to Europe in August, this time to Belgium from where he traveled to Holland and Germany for Dhamma talks.

This diary does not give all the details of this remarkable tour. It merely gives glimpses of Goenkaji's daily life on the tour.

The author is a Vipassana Teacher and Secretary to Goenkaji. This chronicle was the result of informal notes compiled during the author's travels with Goenkaji during this marathon Dhamma tour.

Goenkaji has not had time to read this diary completely. Any errors in it are solely the responsibility of the author.

Contents

The Caravan of Dhamma
The "Meditation Now" Tour
Goenkaji's Tour of Europe and North America
April 10 to August 15, 2002

Europe: United Kingdom

Day 1-5, April 10-14, Dhamma Dīpa, Hereford
    An Island of Dhamma
    Monuments of Dhamma
    Children and Charcoal
    Mataji's Role
    The Householders and the Monks

Day 6, April 15, Dhamma Dīpa, Hereford / Birmingham / London
    The Price of the Priceless Dhamma

Day 7-8, April 16-17, London
    Spreading the Word
    Proper Care of Dāna

United States of America

Day 9, April 18, London, U.K. / New York
    Across the Atlantic

Day 10-14, April 19-23, New York
    Meeting Organizers
    May All Beings Dwell Without Fear
    Modern Agents of Change and Their Responsibility
    A Businessman's Story
    Spirituality for All

Day 15, April 24, New York / Lenox, Massachusetts
    A Long Journey
    Question Mark

Day 16, April 25, Lenox, Massachusetts
    Noon Interviews

Day 17, April 26, Lenox, Massachusetts / Boston, Massachusetts / Lenox, Massachusetts
Boston
Sigh of Relief

Day 18-25, April 27-25, Lenox, Massachusetts
A Herd of Bison
Vipassana Day
Yoga and Vipassana
Course for Businesspeople and Administrators
Professionals Serving Vipassana
Mundane and Supramundane
Morality in Business
Selfless Love

Day 26, May 5, Lenox, Massachusetts / Dhamma Dharā, Massachusetts / Flanders, New Jersey
A Pleasant Surprise
First Night in the Motor Home

Day 27, May 6, Flanders, New Jersey / Rutgers University, New Jersey
You are the Future

Day 28, May 7, Flanders, New Jersey / Manhattan / Queens, New York
India and China
I must be Strict only to be Kind

Day 29, May 8, Queens, New York / Manhattan, New York / Flanders, New Jersey
Blind Faith, Faith and Interfaith

Day 30, May 9, Flanders, New Jersey / Pennsylvania
Annenberg Center, University of Pennsylvania

Day 31, May 10, Coatsville, Pennsylvania / Lincoln University, Pennsylvania / Unionville, Pennsylvania
Maintain the Purity of the Technique

Day 32, May 11, Coatsville, Pennsylvania / Ashland, Virginia
The Dhamma Caravan

Day 33, May 12, Ashland, Virginia / Charlotte, North Carolina
Keep Walking, Keep Walking

Day 34, May 13, Charlotte, North Carolina
Inspiring the Meditators

Day 35, May 14, Charlotte, North Carolina / Atlanta, Georgia
   Stone Mountain Park, Atlanta

Day 36, May 15, Atlanta, Georgia
   Jesus: A Prince among Saints

Day 37, May 16, Birmingham, Alabama
   Prisoners, One And All
   A Dual Responsibility
   True Correction
   Opening the Mind, Opening the Heart
   The Prisoner Inside

Day 38, May 17, Birmingham, Alabama / Houston, Texas
   Houston: Airborne Again

Day 39, May 18, Dhamma Sirī, Kaufman, Texas
   Dhamma Sirī (Wealth of Dhamma)
   Addiction
   Is a Teacher Necessary?

Day 41, May 20, Dhamma Sirī, Texas / Ole Town Cotton Gin RV Park, Texas
   Farewell to Dhamma Sirī
   Journey to Boulder

Day 42, May 21, Texas / Capulin, New Mexico
   Just as in the Sky Different Winds Blow

Day 43, May 22, Capulin, New Mexico / Boulder, Colorado
   Sleeping Volcano

Day 44, May 23, Boulder, Colorado / Denver, Colorado
   Sleepless in Failure, Sleepless in Success
   Mataji Keeps Busy
   Nature Plays Anicca

Day 45, May 24, Boulder, Colorado
   Real Security is Inside
   Illness and Vipassana

Day 46, May 25, Boulder, Colorado
   The Gift of Dhamma Surpasses All Gifts

Day 47, May 26, Boulder, Colorado / Manhattan, New York
   New York: The Sāvatthi of the Modern Age

Day 48, May 27, Manhattan, New York
  A Day of Recuperation
Day 49, May 28, United Nations, New York
  Buddha: A Super-Scientist of Peace
Day 50, May 29, New York / San Diego, California
  Coast to Coast
Day 51, May 30, San Diego, California
  Visit to a Laboratory
Day 52, May 31, Orange County, California
  Questions
  Siddhartha's Quest
Day 53, June 1, Azusa, California
  Myanmar Monastery
Day 54, June 2, Azusa, California
  Sangha Dana
Day 55, June 3, Azusa, California / Dhamma Mahāvana, California
  Khanti (Tolerance)
Day 56-57, June 4-5, Dhamma Mahāvana, North Fork, California
  Dhamma Mahāvana
  Like a Mother Hen Looking After Her Chicks
  Be Like a Lotus
Day 58, June 6, Dhamma Mahāvana, North Fork / Saratoga Springs Campground, California
  Saratoga Springs
Day 59, June 7, Saratoga Springs Campground / Cupertino, California
  Peace Amid Chaos
  Weekend Spirituality
Day 60, June 8, Saratoga Springs Campground / Berkeley / Anthony Chabot Regional Park, Oakland, California
  Silicon Valley Professionals
  Mental Pollution in the Office
  Not Merely to Satisfy Curiosity
  Mind-washing
Day 61, June 9, Oakland / Jain Temple, Milpitas / Hayward / Petaluma, California
  Vīra and Mahavīra: A Warrior and a Great Warrior

Walk the talk
Day 62, June 10, Santa Rosa, California
  Suffering Defined
  From Cruelty to Compassion
  Goenkaji, Start a Vipassana Center Here!
Day 63, June 11, Santa Rosa, California / Albion, California
  Training Under Sayagyi U Ba Khin
  Aware Outside, Aware Inside
  Supernatural Powers
Day 64, June 12, Albion, California / Fort Bragg, California / Albion, California
  Eagles Hall
  From Gross to Subtle
Day 65, June 13, Crescent City RV Park, California
  Minor Accident, Major Delay
  Ancient Tree, Ancient Tradition
Day 66, June 14, Glenyan Campground, Ashland, Oregon
  To Warmer Climes
Day 67, June 15, Ashland, Oregon
  Within This Fathom-Long Body
Day 68, June 16, Ashland / Portland, Oregon
  Long Days, Short Nights
Day 69, June 17, Dhamma Kuñja, Washington
  Grove of Dhamma
  The First Dip in the Ganges of Inner Reality
Day 70, June 18, Dhamma Kuñja, Washington / Portland, Oregon / Dhamma Kuñja, Washington
  Noble Silence
  Ashoka: A Shining Star in the Galaxy of Rulers
  Everyone Has a Seed of Enlightenment
  Escape Is No Solution
Day 71, June 19, Dhamma Kuñja, Washington / Lacey, Washington
  Know Thyself
  Meditation Postures
  Instant Justice

Day 72, June 20, Seattle, Washington
    Recipe for Success, Recipe for Misery
    Recipe for Happiness, Recipe for Success
    Proper Charity
    Meditation and Cults

Day 73, June 21, Seattle, Washington
    Knock Out Punch
    Dhamma in Town Halls
    Outer Shell and Inner Essence

Day 74, June 22, Seattle, Washington
    Dhamma Prison
    Neither Mahayana nor Hinayana: Dhammayana

Canada

Day 75, June 23, Seattle, Washington / Vancouver, British Columbia
    A Gurudwara in Canada
    Dharma is Not for Power, it is for Purity

Day 76, June 24, Vancouver, British Columbia
    No Guru This
    The Clock of Vipassana Has Struck
    A Deep Surgical Operation

Day 77, June 25, Vancouver, British Columbia
    Broadcasting Dhamma
    The Eightfold Noble Path
    Suññatā (Shunyatā)

Day 78 June 26,, Vancouver, BC / Victoria, British Columbia
    Dāna of Food

Day 79, June 27, Victoria, British Columbia
    What Goenkaji Does on a Scheduled Rest Day

Day 80, June 28, Victoria, BC / Chilliwack, British Columbia
    Ambitious Plan

Day 81, June 29, Chilliwack, BC / Dhamma Surabhi, Merritt
    The Fragrance of Dhamma

Day 82, June 30, Dhamma Surabhi, Merritt
    Peace First: The First Nations

Day 83, July 1, Dhamma Surabhi, Merritt / Golden, BC
   Into Nature
Day 84, July 2, Golden, BC / Calgary, Alberta
   The Mighty Rockies
Day 85, July 3, Calgary
   Stampede
   Committed Relationships: Doors are Closed
   Meditation versus Vipassana
   With Eyes Closed
   The Breath: A Bridge to the Unknown
   Peace Within First
Day 86, July 4, Calgary / Edmonton, Alberta
   The Northern Point of the North American Tour
Day 87, July 5, Edmonton, Alberta / High River, Alberta
   Success Without Dhamma Means Ego and Intolerance
   Mosquito Misery

United States of America

Day 86, July 6, High River, Alberta, Canada / Whitefish, Montana
   Rockies Again
   Deer Park
Day 89, July 7, Whitefish / Missoula, Montana
   Open Sky
Day 90, July 8, Missoula, Montana
   Rain and Sunshine
Day 91, July 9, Missoula / Billings, Montana
   Mind Matters Most
Day 92, July 10, Billings, Montana / Bismarck, North Dakota
   Staying Together
Day 93, July 11, Bismarck, North Dakota / Minneapolis, Minnesota
   Longest Day and Another Flat Tire
Day 94, July 12, Minneapolis, Minnesota
   Twin Cities
   Craving: A Bottomless Bucket.
   Anicca to Anattā: A natural progress

Day 95, July 13, Minneapolis, Minnesota / Chicago, Illinois
   Why Vipassana Centers?
Day 96, July 14, Chicago, Illinois
   Sthitaprajña: From a Distant Dream to a Real Possibility
   Field Museum
   Bargain
   Middle Path
Day 97, July 15, Chicago, Illinois
   Separation
Day 98, July 16, Chicago, Illinois
   Essence of Buddha Dhamma
   A Contradiction in Terms
Day 99, July 17, Chicago / Madison, Wisconsin / Chicago, Illinois
   Vipassana Centers
   Vipassana for Leaders
   A Universal Way to Alleviate Universal Misery
   Defiling Impulses
Day 100, July 18, Chicago, Illinois / Brighton, Michigan
   Healthy Habit

Canada

Day 101, July 19, Brighton, Michigan, USA / Toronto, Ontario
   A Second Time in Canada
Day 102-104, July 20-22, Toronto, Ontario
   Auspicious Day
   Buddha's Teaching in India: Centuries of Darkness and
   Misinformation
   Karma
   Diversity of Toronto
   You Make Your Future!
   Diversity of Toronto
   Ageing
   Death and Dying
   Real Strength
   Success
   Yours to Discover: Ontario and Vipassana

Day 105, July 23, Toronto / Ottawa, Ontario
  Secluded Camping Grounds
Day 106, July 24, Ottawa, Ontario
  The Wheel of Dhamma Rotates
  Meeting the Prime Minister of Canada
Day 107, July 25, Ottawa / Dhamma Suttama, Quebec
  Into French-speaking Canada
Day 108-110, July 26-28, Dhamma Suttama, Quebec
  First Course in North America
  Wandering Teacher, Focused Mind
  Distributing Peace
  Women in Dhamma
  Be a Good Human Being First
  The Best Advertising is Word of Mouth
  In the Service of Dhamma
  Service is Essential for Progress in Dhamma
  Expanding Center

United States of America
Day 111, July 29, Dhamma Suttama, Quebec / Boston, Massachusetts
  Back in the U.S.A.
Day 112-113, July 30, 31, Boston, Massachusetts
  Caravan Crew
  John Hancock Center
  Charity
  Spiritual Attainments
  Talk at MIT
Day 114-117, August 1-4, Dhamma Dharā, Massachusetts
  VMC: 20 Years of Service
  The Crew Disperses
  Meeting More Meditators
  One-Day Course
  Packing Up
  Remembering Goenkaji (Smith College)
Day 118-119, August 5-6, Manhattan / Queens / Manhattan
  Monkey Mind
  Exhibition Gallery of the Global Pagoda

Day 120, August 7, New York / London / Brussels, Belgium
  India's Role in the Spread of Dhamma

Europe: Belgium, Holland, Germany
Day 121-124, August 8-11, Dhamma Pajjota, Belgium
  Arrival in Europe
  Violence and Strict Disciplinary Action
  Not 'My' Centers
  Infirm Body, Firm Mind
  Will Vipassana Last?
  Largest Ever Course Outside of South Asia
  A European Union—Unity Amongst Meditators
Day 125, August 12, Dhamma Pajjota, Belgium / Vught, Holland / Dhamma Pajjota, Belgium
  Spirituality in Business, But Not Business in Spirituality
Day 126, August 13, Dhamma Pajjota, Belgium / Cologne, Germany / Dhamma Pajjota, Belgium
  Congress Hall, Cologne
Day 127, August 14, Dhamma Pajjota, Belgium
  Another Ten-Day Course Begins
Day 128, August 15, Dhamma Pajjota, Belgium
  Meeting at European Union
  Chocolate Icing on the Dhamma Tour Cake

Diary of
S. N. Goenka's "Meditation Now" Tour
Europe and North America
April 10 to August 15, 2002

The Caravan of Dhamma
The "Meditation Now" Tour
Goenkaji's Tour of Europe and North America
April 10 to August 15, 2002

Day 1, April 10, Dhamma Dīpa, Hereford, U.K.
An Island of Dhamma
"*Jarā'pi dukkhā, jarā'pi dukkhā.* Old age is misery, old age is misery," said Goenkaji as he got out of his car at *Dhamma Dīpa*, the Vipassana center in Hereford. This was the first stop of his ambitious four-month tour of the West. He showed no signs of feeling miserable, though, as he smiled at the small welcoming party waiting for him. "Are you all happy?" he asked, before anyone could ask about his journey. Without waiting for an answer, he continued, "You must be. You are staying on the Island of Dhamma—*Dhamma Dīpa*."

It had taken Goenkaji and Mataji more than 16 hours to reach here.

Day 2, April 11, Dhamma Dīpa, Hereford
Monuments of Dhamma
It was a cold but sunny early spring day in the southwest of England. The two cherry trees in front of the female dormitory were both in full blossom.

A large number of meditators and their families came to meet with Goenkaji in the afternoon.

Later, in his concluding address to the annual meeting of European assistant teachers, Goenkaji said, "All of you are representatives of Dhamma. People will look at your life to judge Vipassana."

Two qualities are rare in human beings: *pubbakārī* (genuine selflessness in serving others) and *kataññū, katavedi* (gratitude).

Pubbakārī: helping others without expecting anything in return; without expecting money or name or fame. You are here to serve others.

Sometimes, you may not expect money or name or fame but you expect respect. Or you develop arrogance. This is very harmful for you.

A branch of a tree that bears fruit comes down, due to the weight of the fruit. Similarly a person who develops *paññā* (wisdom) becomes more humble.

You got this technique because the Buddha discovered it, after developing so many *pāramīs* over such a long time; because the Sangha preserved it in its purity through the millennia; and because Sayagyi U Ba Khin, my teacher, had such a strong volition that Vipassana should go to India and then spread around the world.

I expressed my doubt to my teacher after he asked me to teach Dhamma in India." Sir, how can an ordinary householder like me, an ordinary businessman, teach Dhamma? And that too in a country where hardly anybody knows me?" Sayagyi U Ba Khin laughed aloud and said, "Don't worry. You are not going, I am going." Since my first course, every time I teach Anapana, I start by saying, "O teacher, I am teaching Dhamma on your behalf." Again, when I teach Vipassana, I say, "I am giving Dhamma as your representative." You all are also representatives of Sayagyi U Ba Khin.

I started the Global Pagoda project in Mumbai in India not only to have a huge meditation hall along with an educational display, but also as a memorial to the Buddha, as a symbol of gratitude to Myanmar, as a symbol of gratitude to Sayagyi U Ba Khin. The pagoda will play an educational role, and help in informing people of the truth about the Buddha.

The Buddha said "*Sukhā saṅghassa sāmaggī, samaggānaṃ tapo sukho.*" It is happiness when meditators gather together, and happiness it is when they meditate together. You are all meditating together here—such great happiness. The Global Pagoda will provide this opportunity to thousands of meditators.

More importantly, you should all understand that each one of you is a monument of Dhamma. Each one of you is a memorial to Sayagyi U Ba Khin. Every single meditator is a memorial. Each meditator should become a lighthouse of Dhamma. This will happen only when you apply Dhamma in life.

Day 3, April 12, Dhamma Dīpa, Hereford
Children and Charcoal

In the morning, Goenkaji was interviewed by the local BBC radio station, and then later also for a BBC World Service radio program. Following these interviews, he spent the rest of the day meeting with individual meditators, trusts from Vipassana centers around Europe, and assistant teachers.

In the evening, Goenkaji gave a public talk at the Shire Hall in St. Peter's Square, in the nearby town of Hereford. The hall was filled to capacity. To create more space, old students (people who had already taken a ten-day Vipassana course) were asked to move to an adjacent room.

Vipassana is a simple and universal technique that benefits one and all by making one aware of what is happening deep inside.

Awareness of reality within is the first step toward changing the unwholesome habit pattern of the mind. Take the example of a child and burning charcoals. The child, out of ignorance, feels that the burning coals are red toys. His mother protects the child by preventing him from approaching them. However, when the mother is not around, the child tries to play with the charcoals. The moment he touches them, he withdraws his hands because they burn him. An ignorant child soon learns that these are burning charcoals that harm him if he touches them. We grown-up people think of ourselves as very knowledgeable but we also make the same mistake! Out of ignorance we keep on generating defilements such as anger, hatred, fear, jealousy, lust. And we keep on burning inside. With the practice of Vipassana we learn to be aware of what happens inside, and by repeated observation and awareness, by repeated practice, we learn to eradicate the defilements that burn us.

Following the talk, some local newspaper reporters interviewed Goenkaji. They were curious about this new mental training technique that was being taught locally.

One reporter asked Goenkaji, "For those who believe in God, it is the God Almighty who is going to give them good qualities; to make them compassionate, etc. You, on the other hand, ask the individual to take the responsibility to purify his or her own mind. Why not just pray to God to do it?" With a smile, Goenkaji answered, "God helps those who help themselves! Learn to help yourself in the right way, by not corrupting your mind, and you will find that you are getting help from every direction."

Day 4, April 13, Dhamma Dīpa, Hereford

Mataji's Role

Meditators from all over Europe had gathered at *Dhamma Dīpa* to join a one-day Vipassana course. Goenkaji gave Vipassana instructions to the more than 400 assembled meditators.

Later in the day, he gave private interviews to meditators and spoke with two journalists.

One of the journalists asked Goenkaji why Mataji willingly accompanies him and helps him on his arduous tours. Goenkaji replied that it is because she wants to share the benefits that she has gotten from Vipassana with others. She assists Goenkaji by practicing *mettā* while he gives Dhamma talks and answers questions, to create a more conducive Dhamma atmosphere. Also, in view of the many past cases of spiritual teachers and gurus exploiting their female disciples, Mataji's presence alongside Goenkaji has always inspired confidence in women. In India, women who don't feel comfortable discussing their personal problems with Goenkaji, out of modesty or other reasons, often talk to Mataji instead. She helps in many other ways, too, such as caring for Goenkaji's personal needs. Furthermore, her presence helps dispel a widely held misconception (especially in India) that the Buddha's teaching is not suitable for householders.

Day 5, April 14, Dhamma Dīpa, Hereford
The Householders and the Monks

Goenkaji is carrying the torch of a tradition that is, today, primarily a householders' tradition. Many of his students are keen to bring their families to meet with Goenkaji, and naturally, meditators with young children want to bring their little ones to sit with him. So, this morning, Goenkaji put aside some time to meet with his students' families.

The big event of the day, however, was *Sangha Dāna*. The Sangha, or monastic tradition, is the repository of the Dhamma. Over the last two millennia it has maintained the Dhamma as a living tradition. Through the centuries, dedicated *bhikkhus* passed down the teaching in all its purity, in an unbroken chain from teacher to pupil, without compromising its universal application and universal appeal. It is thanks to their efforts that we have this wonderful technique today. It is only natural, that those who benefit from Vipassana feel gratitude towards the Sangha for this. They also feel respect for all the members of the Sangha who have renounced everything to dedicate their lives to practicing the Buddha's teaching. Many venerable monks from around Britain were invited to *Dhamma Dīpa* on this day, to be honoured with a meal and traditional gifts of monks´ requisites.

Hundreds of lay people gathered for the opportunity to serve the invited monks and thereby gain merits.

In an address to the gathering, Goenkaji recalled how he was attracted to the teaching because of his saintly teacher, Sayagyi U Ba Khin, because Dhamma gives result "here and now," because of the non-sectarian nature of the Dhamma, and because he could find nothing whatsoever to object to in the teaching of the Buddha.

Day 6, April 15, Dhamma Dīpa, Hereford / Birmingham / London
The Price of the Priceless Dhamma
When Vipassana first began taking root in the U.K., there was a small but dedicated group of students in the Birmingham area. Goenkaji had accepted an invitation to speak at the University of Birmingham during this tour.

As he always does in his discourses, Goenkaji exhorted the audience to give a trial to Vipassana.

There is no price for the teaching, or for the lodging and board at the Vipassana courses, but nevertheless, you have to pay a price. And that price is: Ten valuable days of your invaluable life!

It was almost 9 p.m. when Goenkaji left Birmingham, so he didn't arrive in London until after midnight. During his visit to London, Goenkaji had agreed to stay at the home of Mr. and Mrs. Harshad Patel, who were waiting together with their sons to receive Goenkaji and Mataji. It had been another long day, and this was just the first week of the tour.

Day 7, April 16, London
Spreading the Word
Today, Goenkaji appeared on the Jimmy Young Show on BBC Radio 2. With an average audience of 5 million listeners, this is one of Britain's most popular radio programs. The host was particularly interested in the effect of Vipassana on prisoners and on professionals. Goenkaji was on air for only ten

minutes or so early in the program, but his interview prompted a flood of positive comments and e-mails from listeners throughout the program.

That evening, Goenkaji gave a public talk at the Kadwa Patidar Centre in Harrow, London. He had spoken at the same venue during his last visit to the U.K. It was a very multicultural audience, which included a large contingent from Indian community. Goenkaji spoke in English for 30 minutes and then in Hindi for 30 minutes.

Religion without spirituality is like an empty container from which the nectar has leaked out. It is like a lighthouse that has no light. So many conflicts are due to attachment to the outer shell of religion, while ignoring the valuable inner core, which is universal and common to all the religion.

Dhamma is a way of learning how not to harm oneself and how not to harm others. It is a way to come out of misery. For this, one has to have control over the mind and purity of the mind.

Many of you may have heard the story of Duryodhana from the Mahabharata. Duryodhana used to say, "I know quite well what is right but what to do, I don't have the inclination for it. And I know quite well what is wrong, but what to do, I have the inclination for it." We are all like Duryodhana. We know at the intellectual level what is right, but we still keep on repeating the same mistakes because our mind is not under our control, because it is not pure.

Saints know how important it is to know oneself. A Muslim saint of Punjab—a saint is a saint, whether Muslim, Hindu, Sikh, Christian or Jewish—said, "Unless you know yourself, you cannot know God."

All saints have been teaching people to live a peaceful and happy life. The Buddha gave a practical path to achieve this. Modern science is researching the truth outside. However, the Buddha said that within this fathom-long body you find the truth—the cause of our misery and the way out of misery.

Day 8, April 17, London
Proper Care of Dāna

Goenkaji gave Vipassana instructions at a one-day Vipassana course for old students held at the Kadwa Patidar Hall, London.

He spoke to trustees, teachers and senior Dhamma workers in the evening. In his talk, he stressed that they should take great care with the expenses at Vipassana centers. Even if a center receives a large sum of donations, it should still be very careful with its expenses. Extravagant spending at one center is likely to be copied by other centers. Teachers and trustees should focus on developing the most essential facilities first, and all trusts should try their best to avoid taking big loans. Goenkaji said that one should take greater care with *dāna* (donations) than with one's own money.

Day 9, April 18, London, U.K. / New York, U.S.A.
Across the Atlantic

Goenkaji and Mataji flew to New York in the morning. On arrival at the airport they were received by a small group of Vipassana students. Accommodation for the members of the touring party was arranged at different places around the New York City area, so it took considerable time for everyone to settle down for the evening.

Day 10, April 19, New York
Meeting Organizers

Goenkaji took the chance to catch up with pressing correspondence that had accumulated over the previous two weeks. He responded to a large number of messages from all over the world. In the evening, he gave interviews to the organizers of the *Spirit in Business* conference and some other meditators. Bennet Miller, a Vipassana student and award-winning documentary film maker, met briefly with Goenkaji to discuss his plan to film the North American tour. Eilona Ariel of Karuna Films was also present for the meeting.

Day 11, April 20, New York
May All Beings Dwell Without Fear

Hundreds of local meditators gathered on this rainy day at the Borough of Manhattan College, to join a one-day meditation course. After personally giving the Vipassana instructions, Goenkaji left to visit the scene of last year's tragic terrorist attack in lower Manhattan, just a few minutes drive from the one-day course venue. Practicing *mettā bhāvanā*, Goenkaji chanted (in Hindi), *"Isa mahānagara ke sāre prāṇī sukhī surakṣit hoya re."* (May all beings of this great city be happy and secure.)

Day 12, April 21, New York
Modern Agents of Change and Their Responsibility

In the morning, Goenkaji delivered the keynote speech at the *Spirit in Business* conference at the Hotel Sheraton New York in Manhattan. He began by defining spirituality, and then went on to explain why spirituality is so important for businesspeople.

At one time kings had most of the power and were the biggest influence on society. Now the politicians, administrators and businesspeople have that position of influence. Good and bad qualities percolate from the top. Therefore, it is very important that businesspeople live a moral and righteous life, for their own good and for the good of others.

For a religion, spirituality is a must, but for spirituality an organized religion is not a must. Spirituality doesn't require sectarian crutches. However, for any religion, a base of spirituality is mandatory. Religion becomes lifeless without spirituality. It becomes like an empty vessel, studded with precious stones, which may look beautiful from outside, but from which the nectar [of spirituality] has drained out; like a huge magnificent lighthouse engulfed in darkness, without any light within. How can it show the right path to people?

The Buddha taught how to develop the four sublime qualities of *karuṇā, muditā, upekkhā* and *mettā*. When one sees a miserable person, instead of thinking that it's his own doing or his own karma, one generates compassion—*karuṇā*. When one sees a successful and happy person, instead of developing jealousy one develops sympathetic joy—*muditā*. When one faces an adverse situation, instead of losing the balance of the mind, one remains calm and equanimous—*upekkhā*. And one feels selfless love for all beings everywhere—*mettā*. These are the qualities of a spiritual person.

Every businessman should try to develop these qualities for his own good as well as for the good of others.

Goenkaji expressed joy that so many from the next generation of businesspeople were showing keen interest in spirituality.

Later, Goenkaji gave press interviews on the conference in his room. He was also interviewed by a team from a Dutch television station, regarding the technique of Vipassana.

In one of these interviews, Goenkaji was asked to comment on the issue of celibacy for Catholic clergy, and the prevailing media focus on allegations of misconduct by priests within the church. Goenkaji explained that Vipassana is a tool that has helped large numbers of people to live a celibate life, naturally, by enabling them to face lust in a skillful, balanced way—avoiding the extremes of suppressing it and giving it free license. Vipassana deals with lust at the root level of the mind, where it arises. Every Catholic priest should aspire to cultivate the qualities of Jesus in his life—Vipassana is a tool that makes it easy to do so.

Day 13, April 22, New York
A Businessman's Story

When Goenkaji and Mataji arrived in New York, it was warm and humid—almost oppressively so. However, after a rapid drop in temperature, it became cold.

Since Goenkaji's residence was close to Central Park, he was able to take his morning walk there.

Later in the morning, he returned to the Hotel Sheraton to give some more interviews to media representatives. In the afternoon he delivered a talk on Vipassana and Anapana to the conference participants. The room where he gave the talk was filled to capacity. After talking about Vipassana courses, Goenkaji told his own story—how Dhamma brought so much harmony in his life, how his relationship with his workers improved, and how he started sharing his profits with them.

Vipassana helped me to face the vicissitudes of life. When businesses were nationalized in Myanmar, instead of feeling depressed and dejected, I felt joy—that now I could give more time to Dhamma. On the day when the businesses were suddenly nationalized, I came home and started working on an article on Dhamma. I felt carefree. Thus I saw for myself how the biggest financial loss could not shake **me**. Dhamma gave me the strength to remain unshaken in the face of the vicissitudes of life.

Following his talk, some of Goenkaji's students from the 70's who have now started teaching on their own came to pay their respect to him. Goenkaji was pleased to see them again and happy at their worldly success.

Day 14, April 23, New York
Spirituality for All

On the last day of the conference, Goenkaji again talked about spirituality in business.

In my part of the world, in the past, if a natural calamity such as famine, etc. befell a state, people would often blame it on the king, saying that the subjects have to face adverse consequences because the king was immoral. The king would then undertake to live an upright and righteous life.

It is said, "As the king is, so the subjects will be." Therefore, the leaders of society have a greater responsibility. They also have a greater opportunity to influence others.

When I started taking the first steps on the path of Dharma, I learned from experience that spirituality is not **the** domain of any particular class of society. A priest or a laborer; an academician or an illiterate person; a billionaire or a poor person—all could be equally spiritual.

No other people have to interact with society as much as businesspeople and political leaders. Businessmen have to deal with staff, factory labor, customers, government agencies, etc. As they become more spiritual their behavior becomes gentler, and they start winning over people. Business requires a sharp mind to be able to take quick decisions. When the mind is calm and unperturbed, it takes better decisions.

Spirituality and good business go hand in hand. Both contribute not only to the well-being of owners, shareholders, staff and customers but, equally important, to the real happiness of the businessman himself.

A businessman is always in a relentless race to earn more and more money. At some point, he also starts feeling that now along with money he must also start earning name and fame. And to fulfill this desire, he or she starts giving money in charity. Such charity cannot give him joy. Giving donations or charity is a sublime art. True charity is done without expecting anything in return. One gives away money or serves others to deflate one's ego, not to inflate one's ego. The whole attitude should be how to serve more and more people. That is all.

Day 15, April 24, New York / Lenox, MA.

A Long Journey

Unforeseen delays, including traffic jams, prolonged the trip from New York to the site of the special ten-day Vipassana course for executives at the Eastover Resort in Lenox, Massachusetts. Due to heavy traffic, the motor home in which Goenkaji would be traveling throughout North America was not able to arrive in time at the arranged meeting point—the Welcome Center for Connecticut State. In view of the delay, everybody in the touring party decided to eat a picnic lunch outdoors. Eventually, the motor home managed to break free of the traffic snarls and reached the Welcome Center at around 3:00 p.m.

Question Mark

This was Goenkaji's first taste of riding in the motor home. He soon discovered that the swaying motion of the vehicle at the rear, where the beds were positioned, made it impossible to rest while the vehicle was in motion. This placed a big question mark over the tour, as the entire schedule had been based on the assumption that Goenkaji would be able to take rest while the motor home was moving.

On the other hand, the road today was particularly winding, and the driver was not aware of the swaying at the back. He was still inexperienced with the vehicle as well. Goenkaji was told that the roads would be straighter for the rest of the tour, as the route mainly followed highways. He suggested that handles be fitted next to the beds, so that he and Mataji could grab them for support if the vehicle swayed too heavily.

The tour organizers were all a little concerned, and waited anxiously to see how the ride to Boston would go.

Goenkaji did not reach the Eastover Resort until late in the evening. It had been a long day, involving a lot of packing and unpacking, and many unanticipated stops on the road. By the end of the day everyone was feeling quite tired.

Goenkaji, though, had no time to rest, as he had to prepare quickly to give the Anapana instructions to commence the course for business executives and public administrators. After the Anapana session, the students left the hall and a brief *mettā* session was held for all the Dhamma workers serving the course.

Day 16, April 25, Lenox, MA

Noon Interviews

It was cold but sunny as Goenkaji set out for his customary morning walk. When he is traveling Goenkaji is often accompanied on his walks by one or more long-time students or assistant teachers. This gives him an opportunity to discuss local Dhamma activities, and, when he is at a Vipassana center, to inspect facilities. Here also, Goenkaji was accompanied by a local teacher on his morning walk.

"Day One" of the course for executives at the Eastover Resort was hectic, as students had not yet settled in. The course was being led by John and Gail Beary, Goenkaji's longest-serving assistant teachers. Many other assistant teachers and Dhamma workers had worked hard to prepare the facility for staging the course. Preparing for "non-center" courses involves much more work than preparing for courses at permanent meditation centers, because temporary sites are not equipped with all the required facilities, equipment and signs, etc. At a center everything is usually ready and in place. One difficult task, for example, is to plan the movement of male and female students and create separate pathways to ensure proper segregation. Many new signs for the notice boards also need to be made.

Goenkaji decided to continue his customary practice of offering private interviews to students at 12 noon. Whether staying at a center or a non-center course site, he has always made himself available at this hour to meet with meditators who come individually or in groups for clarification about their practice or guidance on organizational matters. Over the last three decades, Goenkaji has met thousands of meditators, as well as non-meditators, during these noon interviews.

Day 17, April 26, Lenox, MA / Boston, MA / Lenox, MA
Boston

Goenkaji and Mataji made a trip to Boston for a scheduled public talk at the auditorium of Brookline High School. Due to the excessive swaying at the rear of the vehicle, they sat in the front of the motor home for the entire three-hour drive. The vehicle stopped only once along the way, to allow Goenkaji to stretch a little.

Local meditators had arranged to provide home-cooked food for Goenkaji and Mataji and the servers traveling with them. The rendezvous with the meditators took place in the parking area of a public garden. It was close to 2 p.m. when Goenkaji ate his lunch.

A good number of Boston-area meditators had encouraged their friends and relatives to take the opportunity to hear Goenkaji speak. Seeing loved ones listen intently to the simple, practical and liberating wisdom of Dhamma brought joy to their hearts. After the talk, some of the parents of Goenkaji's students came "backstage" to greet and chat with the visiting teacher.

In the question-and-answer session that concluded the talk, Goenkaji was asked how meditators can attract their parents to Vipassana. He said, "By your own example. Be a good son, be a good daughter. Be a good human being. When your parents see that you are leading a peaceful and happy life they will certainly be attracted to Dhamma. The peace and harmony in you will attract them to Dhamma. You must make sure that you serve your parents. It is your first Dhamma, your first duty."

Goenkaji ate dinner in his motor home before heading off. It was after midnight when he arrived back at the Eastover Resort.

Sigh of Relief

Today's trip to Boston had been much smoother than the travels of previous days. Careful driving, straighter roads and the handles fitted to the beds all helped in this. With this success, the organizers heaved a sigh of relief. They now felt confident that they could press ahead without needing to make any major changes to their demanding itinerary.

Day 18, April 27, Lenox, MA.

A Herd of Bison

Due to the excessive travel time (about three hours each way), Goenkaji decided against going to a one-day Vipassana course for old students in Boston. This meant that Goenkaji was able to hold private interviews with many of the executive course students though the afternoon.

All the while, a stream of old students from the region arrived at the resort for the rare chance to meet their teacher.

Some of them traveled for hours just for the chance of a few minutes with him.

While Goenkaji was out on his evening walk he spotted a herd of bison (North American buffalo) that had approached the resort to graze. He was informed that while these animals were common throughout North America at one time, they were killed in such numbers that it was rather rare to see them nowadays, particularly in the eastern United States.

Day 19, April 28, Lenox, MA
Vipassana Day

Whenever Goenkaji is present on the fourth day of a ten-day course, he usually elects to lead the all-important Vipassana session himself. As expected, here at Eastover he gave the Vipassana instructions live in the hall.

Throughout the tour, many people who had never been able to meditate in Goenkaji's presence, despite having taken a large number of Vipassana courses with his assistant teachers, found themselves with the happy opportunity of taking Anapana and/or Vipassana instructions from him directly—either in a one-day course or a ten-day course.

For the first three to four days of a ten-day course, students practice Anapana meditation, to pacify and sharpen their mind—an essential preparation for the effective practice of Vipassana. Quite naturally, a distinct sense of anticipation and excitement hangs in the air on Day 4, in the hours leading up to the Vipassana session. When a person learns Vipassana for the first time, a door opens into the truth within. Goenkaji often describes this as taking one's first dip in the "Ganges of Dhamma." One who receives this priceless instruction directly, in person, from such eminent Vipassana teachers as Goenkaji and Mataji is truly fortunate.

Day 20, April 29, Lenox, MA.

Yoga and Vipassana

Goenkaji's health was a major concern during the planning stage of the current tour. The schedule was becoming tighter and tighter as new engagements were added along the way. Today his assistants felt that they might have to cancel an interview. Goenkaji, however, insisted on fulfilling the commitments he had made. A reporter from the Boston Globe arrived in the morning for the interview.

After the midday interviews with students Goenkaji held a brief meeting with the volunteers serving on the course.

In the evening, Goenkaji gave a talk at the Krupalu Yoga Center, one of the largest yoga centers in the U.S.

The ancient country of India gave two invaluable gifts to the world—yoga and Vipassana. Yoga is practiced around the world by people from all religious and socio-cultural backgrounds for physical health. Vipassana too is being increasingly accepted around the world by people from diverse backgrounds. Neither of these techniques involves any conversion from one organized religion to another organized religion.

The audience put many questions to Goenkaji. When asked if it was necessary to take a full ten-day course, Goenkaji chuckled. "This is the age of instant products and instant spirituality," he replied. "But, to work at the deepest levels of mind, continuity of practice is needed. One gets results immediately and at all times, but one has to work sincerely for it."

Another person asked about the importance of meditating together. Goenkaji explained, "It is important to meditate alone and also important to meditate in a group. Both have their advantages. When one takes a serious long course, solitary meditation is essential but it is a great happiness to meditate occasionally with other meditators."

Every word of the Buddha is based on truth that can be directly experienced by anyone who is willing to give it a try.

When the construction of the Global Pagoda at Gorai in Mumbai (Bombay) is complete, it will enable thousands to meditate together. This will allow us to fully experience what the Buddha meant when he said, *sukhā saṅghassa sāmaggī, samaggānaṃ tapo sukho*—great is the happiness when meditators come together, and great is the happiness when they meditate together.

Day 21, April 30, Lenox, MA
Course for Businesspeople and Administrators

Just as Goenkaji returned from giving interviews in the meditation hall the telephone rang. It was the reporter from the Illinois-based magazine Wellness. Goenkaji was scheduled to give a talk at the Wellness center later in the tour and the magazine wanted to carry an interview with him in the issue leading up to the event. Goenkaji talked with the reporter for almost half an hour.

In the late afternoon, a staff photographer from the Boston Globe came to take photographs of Goenkaji and Mataji and the meditation hall that was set up for the executive course.

The course had attracted considerable media attention, due to the unlikely event of many influential businessmen, high-level professionals and administrators taking 10 days out for a retreat of intensive introspection. More than a hundred of them were on the course and working earnestly.

The previous day a reporter had asked Goenkaji if the format and content of Vipassana courses were modified to suit the different kinds of people taking courses, for example, prison inmates and businesspeople. Goenkaji assured him that the format and content are the same for everyone. "The Buddha's teaching is universal. It is equally applicable to all. Human beings are human beings. They become miserable because of the unwholesome habit patterns of the mind. And when they start observing the truth inside, they start breaking that unwholesome habit pattern. I have found that the ten-day format works equally well for all kinds of people."

Day 22, May 1, Lenox, MA.
Professionals Serving Vipassana

Dr. Paul Fleischman, a renowned psychiatrist and Vipassana teacher was entrusted by Goenkaji with framing guidelines to help Vipassana centers and course organizers effectively and responsibly serve people with mental disorders. Along with his wife (also a Vipassana teacher), he came to meet Goenkaji to clarify a number of issues pertaining to this task. Later, Dr. Fleischman also met with Thomas Crisman, a Vipassana teacher who works as an attorney specializing in intellectual property rights, to discuss some organizational matters.

The devoted service of many active professionals such as these has played an essential role in Goenkaji's mission of spreading Vipassana. The teaching of Dhamma does not encourage people to run away from the responsibilities of life. Rather, it enables them to face their responsibilities squarely and deal with them efficiently—all the time enjoying peace of mind.

Day 23, May 2, Lenox, MA.
Mundane and Supramundane

It was now more than three weeks that Goenkaji had been on the road. Naturally, he must make time for mundane matters such as getting a haircut. However busy his schedule may be, he must eventually fit these in. A constant difficulty for the servers who organize Goenkaji's travels is that while these things take time, they never appear on the tour itinerary! Immediately after completing a pre-arranged telephone interview, Goenkaji dashed out for a haircut. He then returned just in time for the noon interviews. A large number of the course participants were already waiting for him in the meditation hall.

In the evening, the owner of the Eastover Resort (rented course site) came with her daughter and one of her managers to meet Goenkaji. They were curious to learn about the meditation course in progress at their facility—that was free of charge, with pure vegetarian food, in total silence at all times, with so many high-powered professional people sitting silently in meditation for hours on end to a gruelling schedule.

At 9 p.m. Goenkaji went to the meditation hall again to answer questions from meditators. While the noon interviews offered during courses are always private, the evening question-and-answer sessions are open to all students. All of the students remained in the hall to listen to Goenkaji's answers to the various questions put forward—some seeking guidance about how to apply Vipassana in life, others about the technique.

One old student (someone who had previously completed a ten-day course) told Goenkaji how much he had already benefited from Vipassana. Whereas he had frequently slept late in the morning, after his first course he rose early every morning so as not to miss his meditation. "Am I getting addicted to Vipassana?" he asked. Laughing, Goenkaji replied, "Something can be called an addiction only if it is harmful. Your regular practice is helpful to you. Therefore it is not an addiction. Don't worry. Keep on meditating every day and keep on living a happy life. When you find that your practice is becoming weak, join a retreat. You may even join as a part-time student."

Another meditator asked whether religious fanaticism and terrorism were the result of particular religious teachings. Goenkaji answered that when a few so-called followers of a religion commit any cruel, inhuman act, they defile the name of that religion. Such people are ignorant because they do not understand the real teaching of their own religion.

Day 24, May 3, Lenox, MA.
Morality in Business
Today was the ninth day of the course, and all the students were meditating seriously.

Through the day, they were allowed to meet with the teachers leading the course. At noon they could seek a private interview with Goenkaji. In addition, a few students that were facing difficulties were brought to Goenkaji to seek his guidance.

Again at 9 p.m. Goenkaji held an open question-and-answer session in the hall. The day before he had said that the students should try to remain aware of sensations even outside the meditation hours—while eating, walking, bathing, etc. Tonight, he was asked whether it was necessary to feel sensations while working in the outside world. In response, Goenkaji had this to say: "No. At this stage you should meditate sitting in the morning and evening. And you should also maintain awareness of sensations during your leisure time. But while you are working or doing any activity that requires mental concentration, give your full attention to the task at hand. Otherwise you will be distracted from your work. During the day, when you realize that some mental impurity is overpowering you, then for just a few seconds try to observe sensations with open eyes, understanding that both the sensations and the impurity are impermanent. Soon your mind will become calm and you will be able to continue the task at hand."

Another student said that in business it is necessary to speak half-truths and sometimes even lies. Goenkaji explained, "It is our greed that makes us believe that we cannot be totally honest in business. If one practices Vipassana, one realizes that honesty is really the best policy. And as one becomes an honest businessman, the word spreads, and business gets even better. And this also helps to improve the overall atmosphere in the business world.

"Once a lawyer joined a course under Sayagyi U Ba Khin. Although he liked Vipassana, he thought that he needed to lie to defend his clients. Sayagyi told him not to lie and instead to defend only those cases where he was convinced that the defendant was innocent. (Though the decision of guilt is not made by a lawyer, he can certainly refuse to tell lies knowingly in court just to defend his client.) The lawyer accepted Sayagyi's advice. Initially he had some difficulties, and his business suffered for a brief period. But even then he was a happier person. Soon, however, the word spread about his honesty, and he started getting more cases than he could handle. He even earned the respect of judges."

Day 25, May 4, Lenox, MA.
Selfless Love
Goenkaji taught the students on the executive course the technique of *mettā* meditation—the meditation of selfless love.

The practice of *mettā* is the logical conclusion of Vipassana meditation. *Mettā* means selfless love or compassionate goodwill—goodwill for all beings. When the old habit of egoism is weakened, even a little, goodwill for others flows naturally from the depths of the mind. Pure, selfless love is love without expecting anything in return. As Goenkaji describes it, "It is always one-way traffic—you just give without expecting anything in return." And when this vibration of goodwill springs from a pure mind, it creates a peaceful and harmonious atmosphere for the benefit of all.

Goenkaji returned to the meditation hall again at noon to meet with students individually and in groups. He also met privately with meditators at his residence in the evening. Following the videotaped evening discourse, Goenkaji gave a brief talk for the course participants. He emphasized that Vipassana cannot be said to have helped one until a real change starts occurring in one's life. He also reminded the executive-meditators that because they occupy an important position in society, they have a responsibility to be a positive influence on society.

Day 26, May 5, Lenox, MA / Dhamma Dharā, MA. / Flanders, NJ
A Pleasant Surprise
Goenkaji left Eastover Resort in the morning after meeting with a few students from the course.

Although Goenkaji was originally scheduled to travel directly to New York/New Jersey, he decided instead to go to *Dhamma Dharā* (Vipassana meditation center in Shelburne Falls, MA.), where a bilingual Hindi/English ten-day course was in progress.

It was Day 9 of the course. The students on the course were pleasantly surprised by the unexpected arrival of their teacher.

Firstly, Goenkaji went to the Dhamma Hall for an hour or so to answer questions for the students. Then, after having lunch, he met with two meditators who wanted to understand the significance of the Global Pagoda project. In the discussion, Goenkaji explained that while it is easy for people to come together to enjoy sensual pleasures or entertainment, it is difficult to come together for any spiritual purpose. And even when people do gather in the name of spirituality, they do so only out of religious fervor—rarely do they meet to really try to purify the mind, without sectarian attachments. The Global Pagoda will offer an opportunity for people from different religious backgrounds to come together and work towards genuine peace and harmony.

It was a long drive from *Dhamma Dharā* to New Jersey. It was after 10 p.m. when Goenkaji reached the RV Park in New Jersey.

First Night in the Motor Home

Though Goenkaji had traveled in his motor home before, this was the first night he spent in it.

Day 27, May 6, Flanders, NJ / Rutgers University, NJ
You are the Future

It was a one-hour drive from the RV Park to Rutgers University, where Goenkaji was due to give a speech. The audience assembled at the Livingston Student Center consisted of both students and academics. During the question-and-answer session, Goenkaji emphasized the importance for the young people of the world to embrace a rational, logical, scientific spirituality that is devoid of blind faith and fanaticism.

After the talk, Goenkaji met a number of people from the audience. He arrived back at the RV Park soon after 10 p.m.

Day 28, May 7, Flanders, NJ / Manhattan / Queens, NY
India and China
It is unfortunate that although the Buddha's benevolent teaching played a major role in the glorious histories of India and China, the essence of the teaching has been lost in the two countries for many centuries. It is Goenkaji's dream that the original and pure teaching of the Buddha spreads far and wide in both of these great nations, as well as in the United States, the global superpower of today. If this happens, the impact on the entire world will be profound. In view of this, the Indian and Chinese expatriate communities in the United States can play a vital role in diffusing Vipassana in their countries of origin. Although the idea of meditation may still be somewhat foreign to the American public, more and more people are being drawn to the practical teaching of the Buddha—because it is universal, non-sectarian, pragmatic and result-oriented.

Goenkaji devoted his morning to Indian expatriates, and most of his evening to Chinese-American meditators.

Goenkaji was invited for an interview to the studio of ITV, a cable TV station serving Manhattan's Indian community. Goenkaji talked of how this long-lost jewel of India, Vipassana, has returned to India and is spreading around the world.

After the interview, Goenkaji traveled to Queens, NY. His motor home was parked for the night near the New York Vihara.

I Must be Strict Only to be Kind
In the evening, Goenkaji dropped in to the Dhamma House in Queens, a permanent venue where local meditators run regular group sittings and one-day courses. A sizable number of Chinese Vipassana students live in this part of New York. Goenkaji arrived at the end of the group sitting and offered to answer questions. One meditator wanted to know why Reiki practitioners were allowed only one Vipassana course.

Reiki and similar healing practices do help people and I have nothing against them. But when such practices are mixed with Vipassana there is danger of harming oneself and harming others. All such practices attempt to alter reality by means of calling on some external force or auto-suggestion (e.g. self-hypnosis). This prevents one from observing the truth *as it is*. Therefore, these practices are fundamentally at odds with the objective observation of reality that is Vipassana.

The purpose of Dhamma is to make one strong and independent. If one depends on an external force, one becomes weak. And it makes one addicted to pleasant sensations that one is not even aware of, much less able to observe objectively. Therefore, one generates subtle but strong *saṅkhāras* (karma) of craving and *moha* (ignorance).

Reiki practitioners can take only one Vipassana course. Then they have to choose one practice—either Vipassana or Reiki. This restriction is not based on speculative reasoning, but on actual experience. I had to take this strong measure, reluctantly, after the experience of many cases around the world in which people harmed themselves by mixing Reiki and Vipassana—even to the point of becoming mentally imbalanced. Many, many Reiki practitioners also started distorting the practice of Vipassana, thereby harming their patients and students, harming themselves, and confusing new students of Vipassana.

We have a serious responsibility towards the well-being of Vipassana students who come to courses. Even if only a few are in danger, we have to be careful. They have learned Vipassana and we have warned them. Now, if they continue to practice both, they are free to do so on their own. But allowing them to continue taking courses would amount to encouragement. I certainly don't want to take that risk. I have to be firm.

Goenkaji usually does not go to restaurants but when he is traveling circumstances sometimes force him to do so. Tonight he ate dinner at a local Chinese restaurant. Although most of the meditators accompanying him were of Chinese origin, other

Vipassana students representing a variety of nationalities joined the group.

Day 29, May 8, Queens / Manhattan, NY / Flanders, NJ
Blind Faith, Faith and Interfaith

There is no place for blind faith in Vipassana. Meditators progressively develop real faith that grows out of their own experience of truth within. This quality is a source of great strength on the path of Dhamma. True faith is accompanied by discriminating wisdom and always keeps one on the right path.

The word "faith" is also often used as a synonym for religion or philosophy. Now, although the *sangha*, or community of *bhikkhus* (monks) is seen by some as a sectarian entity, serious meditators come to realize that they have obtained this priceless jewel only because it was lovingly preserved through the millennia in its pristine, non-sectarian purity by a chain of *bhikkhu-teachers*. For this we are forever grateful to the *sangha*. And remembering this, we can take inspiration and confidence from it. In the Buddha's teaching, *saddhā* means faith or confidence—the confidence that one develops naturally in the teaching of the Buddha from one's own experiential wisdom. It is a conviction borne not just out of devotion or intellectual reasoning, but from the experiential wisdom that one develops by taking practical steps on the path of Dhamma.

At the New York Vihara in Queens, Goenkaji served food to an assembly of the Bhikkhu Sangha headed by Ven. Piyatissa. Dozens of meditators from a wide range of backgrounds joined in this meritorious event. People from India, Sri Lanka, Myanmar, Cambodia, China, Taiwan, Hong Kong, Bangladesh, Thailand, Israel, Europe and North America took the opportunity to serve the *bhikkhus*. Later on the *bhikkhus* were also given gifts of traditional requisites. To conclude, Goenkaji gave an inspiring address. As he often does, he recounted how joyous he felt to see *bhikkhus* out on their morning alms rounds in his motherland of Myanmar—how inspiring to see them walking silently in single file with eyes downcast.

In the afternoon, Goenkaji held private meetings with assistant teachers on organizational matters.

In the evening, Goenkaji gave a talk at the Interfaith Center in Manhattan, an organization that has worked for many decades to bring together people of different faiths. In view of this, it was a highly fitting venue for Goenkaji's message.

Reverend Dean Morton introduced Goenkaji and asked him to speak on the subject of "Dharma and Business." Goenkaji explained that while success and failure, and profit and loss are a natural part of doing business, if one has not learned to maintain equanimity in the mind, these ups and downs inevitably bring about suffering.

After the talk, Goenkaji engaged in media interviews before he headed back to Flanders, arriving there around 11 p.m.

Day 30, May 9, Flanders, NJ / Pennsylvania, PA
Annenberg Center, University of Pennsylvania

The venue for Goenkaji's public talk in the evening was the Zellerbach Theater in the University of Pennsylvania's Annenberg Center. Goenkaji was introduced by Steve Gorn.

Vipassana is a simple, practical way to achieve real peace of mind and to lead a happy, useful life. Vipassana enables us to experience peace and harmony. It purifies the mind, freeing it from suffering and the deep-seated causes of suffering. The practice leads step-by-step to the highest spiritual goal of full liberation from all mental defilements.

Usually, when one faces a difficult situation—say, for example, when one is angry—one is not aware of what is happening inside. One goes on burning and burning. And even if one realizes one is angry, one tends to deal with it by diverting one's attention to something else, perhaps by taking intoxicants or indulging in sensual pleasures. A better approach than this might be to recite something, or to pray, or to try to distract the mind, by counting numbers for example, or to get involved in some other activity. All this is only running away from the problem. We must learn to face the problem rather than running away from it.

But how to face anger? It has no shape or form. A Vipassana meditator comes to realize that with every impurity that arises in the mind there is a flow of sensations on the body. When anger arises, sensations of burning start. One learns to observe these or any other sensations that are felt at this time. One does not dwell on the cause of the anger. One just accepts that there is anger now, and understands, by experiential wisdom, that the sensation is impermanent, and so too is the anger.

Thus, one has learned to face the problem. And as one keeps on observing sensations with equanimity, impurities start to get eradicated from the root of the mind.

Some local meditators kindly led the tour caravan to its stop for the night. After a drive of about one hour, as a soft drizzle fell, the motor homes arrived at the campground in Coatsville, PA. Some of the meditators from the caravan took shelter in the wood cabins at the edge of the campsite.

This was the first day that all the support group of meditators had traveled together with their motor homes and campers. The entire crew of the Dhamma caravan was now together.

Day 31, May 10, Coatsville, PA / Lincoln University / Unionville, PA
Maintain the Purity of the Technique

A one-day course was organized in the Rivero Hall at Lincoln University by the strong group of local old meditators, which includes many of the local Cambodian community.

Goenkaji gave a brief talk at the course.

One of the most important reasons why Vipassana was lost in India, the country of its origin, was that people started adding things to it. The Buddha's teaching is *paripuṇṇam*—it is complete, there is no need to add anything to it. It is *parisuddham*—it is totally pure, there is no need to remove anything from it.

At Vipassana centers, we must take care that we teach nothing but *sīla* (morality), *samādhi* (concentration of mind) and *paññā* (purification of mind). If we start any other activity, even if it looks quite harmless, then that particular activity will become more and more important, and Vipassana may be relegated to a secondary position.

Now that the Buddha's teaching is rising again, let us keep it in its pristine purity, so that it helps more and more people around the world, for centuries to come.

In the evening, Goenkaji gave a talk at the Unionville High School Auditorium. Someone asked Goenkaji what he had to say about love at first sight. Goenkaji laughed, saying, "Why only at *first* sight? There should be love at *every* sight! But it should be pure love. Pure love is full of compassion. It is totally free of lust."

Day 32, May 11, Coatsville, PA / Ashland, VA
The Dhamma Caravan

Many old students had expressed a desire to join the group of vehicles traveling with Goenkaji and Mataji. The tour organizers carefully selected a few of these, based on their utility to the tour. Some became official tour members and some were allowed to join as independent vehicles to provide additional support to the group. All these meditators were assigned various duties, such as serving food, laundry, driving, vehicle maintenance, recording of Goenkaji's public talks and talks to meditators, distributing literature, logistics for various events, and coordination with local organizers. In all, seven vehicles (motor homes and camper vans) made up the Dhamma caravan that was taking Goenkaji around North America to spread the munificent message of Dhamma.

The crew members had volunteered their time for anything from a week up to the whole tour to help in various capacities, looking after Goenkaji and supporting his work as a Dhamma Messenger. Those leaving before the end of the tour would be replaced by other Dhamma servers. The caravan crew consisted mostly of assistant teachers and other very experienced meditators.

The caravan left Pennsylvania at around 10 a.m. and reached its destination at 6 p.m.

Goenkaji had agreed to give a live telephone interview on a Houston radio talk show called "The Open Forum." He gave the interview straight after arriving at the campground, and then answered questions from the radio show audience between 6.30 to 7 p.m.

Due to public talks and other engagements, Goenkaji had missed many of his evening walks over the past month. Today, however, he was able to walk at leisure because it had not yet become dark. These walks are a very important part of his daily routine and help him to keep healthy and fit.

Since there were no pressing jobs for them to do, many of the Dhamma caravan crew could afford to take an hour off at the same time to meditate together.

Day 33, May 12, Ashland, VA / Charlotte, NC
Keep Walking, Keep Walking
The Dhamma caravan had to cover more than 300 miles this day in order to reach Charlotte, North Carolina. This seemed a rather daunting proposition, because motor homes cannot travel at the same speed as a car.

As the vehicles sped along the Interstate 85 South, Goenkaji found time to read and write. Vast expanses of green woodlands on either side of the road were interspersed with fields of colorful flowers and, at times, lakes.

Some of the caravan crew started getting a bit tired of the long journey. Goenkaji, however, sat absorbed in his work. The week before, as he was returning from a public talk and still on the road after 11 p.m., he could be heard chanting:

Cala sādhaka calatā rahe, desh aur pardesh;
Dharma-cārikā se katem, sabake manake klesh.
Keep travelling, O meditator,
In your country and abroad,

By this Dhamma tour,
May everyone's mental impurities be eradicated.

The caravan reached the Charlotte Hindu Center by evening. After attending to all their mundane tasks, such as parking and connecting vehicles to electric power and water supplies, the caravan crew joined with some local meditators for a one-hour group sitting, from 9.30 to 10.30 p.m.

Day 34, May 13, Charlotte, NC
Inspiring the Meditators
In whichever area he happens to visit, Goenkaji's presence revitalizes Vipassana activities. It brings together local old students for meditation, helps them to get to know each other better, and then inspires them to work on spreading Dhamma in the region. Goenkaji's arrival also gives them an opportunity to serve in different capacities at the various organized events. As Emperor Ashoka wrote in one of his edicts, "To do good is difficult. We must try to do good in many different ways." Serving in various capacities complements our practice of meditation.

And so it happened in Charlotte. More and more meditators came forward during the preparations for Goenkaji's visits. It was a joy for all to realize just how many meditators lived in their area. One long-lost old student was a physician who had taken a ten-day course back in 1971. He had called up the local contact person excitedly after hearing somewhere that Goenkaji was coming to Charlotte. Happily, he was able to meet with Goenkaji after the public talk in Charlotte. He reported that the Vipassana course he had taken over 30 years earlier had had a life-transforming effect on him. There was also a woman who had taken a course in 1973. She had brought along her 15-year old son to listen to Goenkaji's discourse.

It was very encouraging for meditators of Charlotte to learn that there were more old students in the area than they had thought. So they are now planning more non-center courses in the region. And since there is no Vipassana center nearby, they are thinking seriously about establishing one in the area.

One local meditator brought his son to Goenkaji's talk. For a long time he had been trying, unsuccessfully, to convince his son to give Vipassana a try. After the talk, for the first time, his son agreed to join a ten-day course.

Day 35, May 14, Charlotte, NC / Atlanta, GA
Stone Mountain Park, Atlanta

Goenkaji and Mataji left the Charlotte Hindu Center in the morning, and by evening, the caravan reached Stone Mountain Park.

Since the caravan volunteers were new to most areas, local meditators met them at the highway exits or nearby rest areas to escort them to their overnight stations.

Every time the caravan reached its destination it took considerable time to find out what facilities are available and to set up the vehicles. Most of the large vehicles needed electrical, water and sewage connections. All vehicles needed electrical hook-ups to charge their mobile phones, two-way radios, and the batteries needed for the various cameras used to document the trip. Communication between vehicles was achieved by the two-way radios or mobile phones, though mobile phone service could be very spotty in more remote parts of the country. Email connections were usually available at the offices of RV Parks.

The Stone Mountain Family Campground was quiet and peaceful. Goenkaji took a long walk on the winding pathways of the campground, while Mataji took the opportunity to inspect the facilities in some of the motor homes in the Dhamma caravan.

Day 36, May 15, Atlanta, GA
Jesus: A Prince Among Saints

In the morning, Goenkaji gave an interview by telephone to Tricycle, an American Buddhist publication. Goenkaji explained that the Buddha's discovery that sensation is the key to liberation from all suffering has been forgotten. So, to clarify our practice it is necessary to go back to the actual words of the Buddha.

Later in the morning, a group of meditators arrived from Atlanta to see Goenkaji at the RV Park. They meditated quietly for some time outside Goenkaji's motor home. Goenkaji and Mataji emerged later to lead a short *mettā* session and speak a few words of encouragement. Later, the visitors were invited to stay for lunch by the caravan crew. The local meditators had brought plenty of food so there was more than enough for all.

In the evening, Goenkaji gave a talk at the Glenn Memorial United Methodist Church at Emory University. "Jesus Christ is a prince among saints," he said.

Jesus had love and compassion for the very people who tortured him to death. This indeed is a sign of a true saint. Goenkaji said that Vipassana would help one to imbibe the qualities of Jesus Christ and apply them in one's life. Vipassana practice involves nothing but the truth that one experiences from moment to moment. 'And ye shall know the truth and the truth shall make you free.'

Goenkaji was asked many questions about the theory and practice of Vipassana.

To the question of why people need Vipassana if they are already happy, Goenkaji replied, "Don't you want to be happier"? He then went on to explain how one is not aware of one's misery. It is like a piece of charcoal that remains hot even though it appears to be cool because of the ash covering it. In a similar way, people delude themselves, failing to recognize their impurities, dissatisfactions, frustrations, anxieties, fears and attachments. How can one be happy when the mind is continually defiled by impurities such as anger, hatred, jealousy, fear, anxiety and greed? Vipassana not only makes you aware of these impurities, it also starts eradicating them.

The next stop on the tour was Birmingham, Alabama. Since he was due to visit the Donaldson Correctional Facility at Birmingham the next morning, Goenkaji decided to make the three-hour trip immediately after the public talk. The caravan left Atlanta at 10 p.m., reaching Birmingham at 1 a.m.

Day 37, May 16, Birmingham, AL
Prisoners, One And All
The Donaldson Correctional Facility in Birmingham, a maximum security prison, held its first Vipassana course in January this year. Today was the final day of the second course in the prison. Goenkaji was welcomed at the gates by Dr. Debra Marshall, a prison psychologist who had been inspired by the potential of Vipassana after taking a ten-day course at *Dhamma Dharā*, Massachusetts.

A Dual Responsibility
Firstly Goenkaji was led to the prison gymnasium, which had been transformed into a temporary meditation hall for each of the courses. Students from both the first and second courses were meditating there. Goenkaji expressed his joy at being able to visit the meditators in prison. Following the group sitting, he gave a short talk. He told the prisoners that in addition to working for their own liberation, the regular practice of Vipassana would help them to fulfill two important responsibilities. Firstly, they would be giving a good example to their fellow inmates, so that they might also be inspired to try Vipassana. Secondly, they would be helping to make the Vipassana program at Donaldson Facility a success, and this, in turn, would make the government take notice. Thus, inmates of other prisons in the country would have a better chance to learn Vipassana. Furthermore, a successful Vipassana program in U.S. prisons would make it easier to implement prison courses in other countries as well.

True Correction
After his brief talk to meditators, Goenkaji met with prison officials including the Deputy Commissioner and Director of Programs of the Alabama Department of Corrections, Dr. Cavanaugh and Mr. Hardison, the prison warden, Mr. Bullard,

and prison psychologist Dr. Marshall. Ms. Phillips of the Lion Heart Foundation also joined the meeting. Goenkaji expressed his appreciation for the initiative demonstrated by all these officials in organizing Vipassana courses at the Donaldson Facility.

Convicted criminals are sent to prison with the aim of correcting their behavior. However, after spending time in the punitive and crime-infested environment that characterizes most prisons, they tend to come out worse than they began. If a prison is to truly live up to its name as a "correctional facility," the inmates must be provided with effective tools to reform themselves, so that they become peaceful and respectable members of society.

Opening the Mind, Opening the Heart

Dr. Marshall described the previous week in the prison as "sensational." She asked three meditators to talk about their experiences in the Vipassana course.

Leon sat his first course in January and served as a volunteer on the second course. He described his experience of sitting the course as "opening the mind" and that of serving as "opening the heart."

Another inmate, Eli, said that Vipassana meditation was very much needed in the prison and that he felt very grateful to have received such a valuable gift.

Rick revealed that he had been imprisoned for 22 years. He had had plenty of time to deal with personal issues during his years in the prison, and he had come to forgive others for his plight. But he was never able to forgive himself. "I kept running away from myself all these years. Finally Vipassana forced me to face my inner self—to look inward. It was the most difficult thing I had ever done but Vipassana gave me the courage and clarity to come to terms with the present reality."

The Prisoner Inside

Goenkaji then gave a brief talk to an assembly of meditators, prison staff and selected inmates who had not yet taken a Vipassana course.

You live within the walls of prison, away from your family, away from the comforts of a home. And this makes you miserable. But there is a greater prison that is the true cause of your misery. People both within and outside of the walls of the prison are prisoners of their unwholesome mental habit patterns. All keep on generating mental impurities such as anger, fear, hatred, jealousy, and greed, which make them miserable. The purpose of Vipassana is to free ourselves from the prison inside.

After Goenkaji's inspiring address, meditator inmates asked him questions about their practice. It was touching to see how Vipassana had reached these people in the most unlikely of places and brought them such comfort.

Day 38, May 17, Birmingham, AL / Houston, TX

Houston: Airborne Again

Since their arrival in the U.S., Goenkaji and Mataji had traveled only by road. This is because air travel has become increasingly difficult for them over the years. However, they decided to brave the skies for a trip to Houston, the fourth largest city in the U.S. They flew in from Birmingham on a morning flight that landed late due to bad weather. It was a one-hour drive from their residence to the city.

Immediately on his arrival Goenkaji met with some local expatriate Indians. Among them were the deputy chairperson of the upper house of the Parliament of India and the Indian consul in Houston.

In the evening, he was interviewed for a radio program before delivering a public talk at the Adam's Mark Hotel. The hall had been set up with 800 chairs, but as more people than expected turned up to hear Goenkaji, the curtain wall at the rear of the hall was removed to make more space and additional chairs were set up.

To learn the technique of Vipassana it is necessary to take a ten-day residential course. In Vipassana, continuity is the secret of success. One starts with observation of breath, which is strongly related to the mind and mental impurities. Once the mind is concentrated to some extent it becomes sharp enough to start feeling sensations—first under the nostrils above the upper lip, and later throughout the body. Soon one starts to realize that one responds to these sensations by generating craving and aversion—and also, that the only way to uproot the impurities in the mind is to maintain clear awareness of these sensations without reacting to them—that is, observing them with equanimity. Just as a poisonous tree will sprout again and again if its roots are not cut out, it is not possible to eradicate mental impurities without working at the level where they arise and multiply.

After the talk Goenkaji traveled to the Southwest Vipassana Center, *Dhamma Sirī*. He and Mataji ate dinner in the car on the way. They reached the center at 1 a.m.

The caravan had driven for 12 hours from Alabama so that they could reach *Dhamma Sirī* in time for Goenkaji and Mataji to spend the night in the motor home.

Day 39, May 18, Dhamma Sirī, Kaufman, TX

Dhamma Sirī (Wealth of Dhamma)

There was heavy rain in both Houston and Kaufman on the previous day, but today the sun shone brightly in a clear sky.

During his morning walk, Goenkaji looked over the facilities of the Vipassana center. He was happy to see that there were many more Dhamma workers at the center than during his last visit here.

At 11 a.m. he met with two senior assistant teacher couples who have continued to serve on many courses despite their advanced age and attendant illnesses. Goenkaji inquired after their health. The teachers in charge of *Dhamma Sirī* then introduced the new board of trustees to Goenkaji. The current trust is composed mainly of young people. The teacher said, "Goenkaji, this is the future of *Dhamma Sirī*." Goenkaji remarked, "Yes, it is good to see that young people coming forward and taking more and more responsibility." After the meeting with the trust, he gave private interviews to many meditators who had converged at the center from near and far. He retired for lunch shortly after 1 p.m.

In the evening, Goenkaji returned to the Dhamma Hall for a question-and-answer session.

Day 40, May 19, Dhamma Sirī, Kaufman, TX / Dallas, TX
Addiction

In the morning, Goenkaji again made himself available at *Dhamma Sirī* to meet meditators, both individually and in groups.

In the evening, he gave a public talk at the beautiful Sara Ellen & Samuel Weisfeld Center in Dallas.

Goenkaji explained how people keep on reacting to sensations without being aware of it.

> The Buddha defined ignorance not as any lack of knowledge about scriptures or philosophical beliefs, but as a lack of awareness of what is happening inside. That is, the lack of awareness of the impermanent and unsatisfactory nature of everything in the field of mind and matter—things over which we have no control.
>
> An alcoholic believes that he is addicted to alcohol. But actually, what he is addicted to are the sensations that he gets when he takes alcohol. After learning Vipassana, it becomes easy to observe the sensations that arise when there is craving—without giving in to unwholesome urges. This is how to start breaking down addictions.
>
> And apart from intoxicants, people are also addicted to different kinds of mental impurities, such as fear, depression and anger. Whenever such defilements arise in the mind, a biochemical flow starts in the body, and this leads to a vicious

cycle of reaction. Vipassana helps to eliminate this habit of blind reaction.

Is a Teacher Necessary?

To a question on whether a teacher is necessary for learning Vipassana, Goenkaji pointed out that in Vipassana there is no "gurudom." In fact, students are cautioned not to get caught in the clutches of any guru. But to learn the technique properly it is important to train under an experienced teacher in a residential course. After the course, the participants become their own masters, and they continue to practice on their own.

Day 41, May 20, Dhamma Siri, Kaufman, TX / Ole Town Cotton Gin RV Park, TX

Farewell to Dhamma Siri

The Dhamma caravan departed from the center at around 11 a.m. Meditators lined up along the driveway to pay respects to Goenkaji and Mataji as the vehicles left the center. During his two-day stay, Goenkaji had managed to meet everyone who had wanted to see him. Tears rolled down Mataji's eyes as she bade farewell to the meditators.

This was Goenkaji and Mataji's first stay at a center in North America during the Meditation Now tour of 2002.

Journey to Boulder

The long journey to Boulder began, with the caravan heading west across the plains of Texas. It would take three days to reach Denver.

In the evening, the caravan stopped at the Ole Town Cotton Gin RV Park. One of the caravan crew bought a picture postcard to post to her grandson. It was a picture of a father and a son driving a truck. The father is telling his son, "Son, the sun has riz and the sun has set, and it is still the Texas state!" And so it was for the caravan. The state of Texas is huge. Even after a long day of driving, the caravan was still well inside the state borders.

Day 42, May 21, Texas / Capulin, NM
Just as in the Sky Different Winds Blow

A strong wind blew as the caravan started out across the vast plains of the Texas Panhandle and New Mexico, staying with the caravan for most of the day. It was at times dusty, at times clear, mostly fierce but occasionally gentle. For long periods it blew from the side, causing the motor homes to sway, thus forcing the drivers to slow down. At times it served as a tailwind, pushing the vehicles to higher speeds. In this flat landscape the sky seemed to stretch forever to the horizon. The wind shook everything in its path. Yet it could not shake the equanimity of the intrepid drivers!

The meditators were reminded of the Buddha's words:
Yathāpi vātā ākāse, vāyanti vividhā puthū;
puratthimā pacchimā cāpi, uttarā atha dakkhiṇā.
Sarajā arajā capi, sītā uṇhā ca ekadā;
adhimattā parittā ca, puthū vāyanti mālutā.
Just as in the sky, different winds blow:
From east and from west, from north and from south,
Dust-laden and dustless, cold and hot,
Fierce gales and gentle breezes—many winds blow.
Tathevimasmiṃ kāyasmiṃ, samuppajjanti vedanā;
sukhadukkhasamuppatti, adukkhamasukhā ca yā.
Yato ca bhikkhu ātāpī, sampajaññaṃ na riñcati.
tato so vedanā sabbā, parijānāti paṇḍito.
So also within the body arise sensations: pleasant, unpleasant or neutral. When a meditator, striving ardently, does not lose his constant thorough understanding of impermanence even for a moment, such a wise person fully comprehends all sensations.
So vedanā pariññāya, diṭṭhe dhamme anāsavo;
kāyassa bhedā dhammaṭṭho, saṅkhyaṃ nopeti vedagū
Having thus comprehended sensations, he becomes freed of all defilements. After death, such a person, being established in Dhamma attains the indescribable state beyond the

conditioned world because he knows sensations thoroughly (their arising and passing away and also the state beyond the sensations).

The caravan arrived finally at the RV Park in Capulin, New Mexico at 7:30 p.m. Capulin is a sleepy, little hamlet of just a few houses. There were a few fierce-looking but friendly dogs around and many large, handsome horses. The owners of the park mentioned that the strong winds were very unusual for this time of year.

As the caravan settled in for the night and the meditators retired to their beds, the wind continued to sway the stationary motor homes throughout the night.

Day 43, May 22, Capulin, NM / Boulder, Co
Sleeping Volcano
In the morning, one enthusiastic crew member took Goenkaji and Mataji to the nearby dormant Capulin Volcano for their morning walk.

All were reminded of Goenkaji's simile of a sleeping volcano to describe *anusaya kilesa*.

In the darkness of ignorance the mind keeps reacting to bodily sensations with craving and aversion. It has become a slave of this deep-rooted behavior pattern. Due to the *anusaya kilesa*, or "sleeping impurities," the mind is like a sleeping volcano that can erupt at any time. The Buddha's great achievement was to find a way to break this blind habit of reacting to sensations. Meditation techniques that ignore sensations cannot possibly take one to the depth of the mind, so they cannot root out mental defilements. With Vipassana, however, the way to eradicate the latent tendencies to craving, aversion and ignorance is clearly spelled out.

In the words of the Buddha:
Sukhāya, bhikkhave, vedanāya rāgānusayo pahātabbo,
dukkhāya vedanāya paṭighānusayo pahātabbo,
adukkhamasukhāya vedanāya avijjānusayo pahātabbo.

Make use of pleasant sensations to eradicate the latent tendency to craving (by equanimous observation of pleasant sensations and clear comprehension of their changing nature); make use of unpleasant sensations to eradicate the latent tendency to aversion, and make use of neutral sensations to eradicate the latent tendency to ignorance.

The caravan took to the road again, rolling across the plains and then up into the mountains of Colorado. Fierce winds continued to blow. Every now and then, wild horses, cows and wild deer could be seen on the sides of the road.

The caravan arrived in Boulder in the evening. All the vehicles were parked in the compound of the house of a meditator couple. Goenkaji briefly met the local assistant teachers and his hosts. The winds remained too strong for Goenkaji to take his evening walk out in the open.

Day 44, May 23, Boulder, Co / Denver, Co
Sleepless in Failure, Sleepless in Success

Goenkaji was invited to speak at a meeting of the Economic Club of Denver, at the Westin Downtown hotel. Goenkaji talked about his life before and after Vipassana. Before taking up Vipassana he had been a highly ambitious businessman. Whenever he would miss a business opportunity or lose a contract he would become agitated and unhappy, to the point of sleeplessness. If he happened to lose out to a competitor, the misery would be even greater. Yet, it was not only when things went wrong that he became miserable. Even after concluding a lucrative deal he would become agitated and sleepless out of excitement—lying awake making further plans for the future and building castles in the air. To a lesser or greater extent, this is how everyone reacts to ups and downs. Though Goenkaji was very successful in his business life, success brought him great stress and tension, which in turn affected the people around him. Through no fault of their own, his wife (Mataji) and children would have to bear the brunt of his frequent eruptions of anger.

In Vipassana, Goenkaji found a tool that helped him not only to enjoy real peace and contentment, but also to work more effectively and efficiently as a businessman and administrator. A sharp and balanced mind makes quick and sound decisions. He also noted that with Vipassana he felt fresh and energetic even after a long workday. He concluded by exhorting the businesspeople in the audience to invest ten days to learn this non-sectarian technique.

Mataji Keeps Busy

With all the long days of travel, Mataji took up some sewing work to pass the time. She also washed some of her sarees—those that could not be done in a washing machine. One of the Dhamma servers offered to take care of all the work that she was doing, but Mataji refused firmly, pointing out that it's a good habit to stay active.

Nature Plays Anicca

It was a bright, sunny and windy evening when the Dhamma caravan rolled in to Boulder. The grounds where the motor homes were parked were lush green. The following morning, the earth was blanketed in white. Every tree and every twig of every tree was dusted with snow.

Day 45, May 24, Boulder, Colorado

Real Security is Inside

In the wake of the September 11 attacks on the World Trade Center towers, questions relating to terror and terrorism were bound to arise during the tour. This question was asked after Goenkaji's talk to a capacity audience in the huge ballroom of the Westin Hotel in Westminster. Goenkaji explained that it was the responsibility of all governments to ensure the security of their populations. As responsible citizens we must all help in this task to the best of our capacity. However, even as the government does its utmost to make our countries safe, we must still confront the issue of fear, because ultimately we must feel secure in our minds. The greatest security lies inside.

Earlier in the talk Goenkaji explained how basic human values are an essential part of all religious teachings, and how without these universal spiritual principles, a religion is like an empty vessel from which nectar has leaked out.

Illness and Vipassana

Goenkaji was asked about the value of Vipassana in facing illness. Illness is as much a part of human existence as birth, old age and death. Naturally, someone afflicted with a disease should seek appropriate professional treatment for it. In some cases, Vipassana may help relieve a disease, if it is psychosomatic in nature. But even when an illness is purely physical, Vipassana is very beneficial, because it trains one to maintain equanimity in the face of unpleasant sensations. That is, it makes it possible to face the pain and discomfort of the disease bravely, with a tranquil mind. There are many cases where a serious Vipassana meditator facing the pains of terminal cancer chooses to take painkillers—since they don't affect awareness of sensations—but refuses medicines that cause drowsiness or dullness in the mind. Knowing that death is imminent, the meditator wishes to remain as conscious and alert as possible, in order to face death squarely with equanimity. Vipassana makes one courageous.

One person in the audience wanted to know whether the good deeds of this life cross over with us to the next life. Answering in affirmative, Goenkaji explained that each of us dies and gets born anew at every moment without interruption. Life is a stream or flow of consciousness that continues from one life to the next, carrying with it our accumulated wholesome and unwholesome deeds.

Day 46, May 25, Boulder, Colorado
The Gift of Dhamma Surpasses All Gifts

Local Vipassana meditators have been holding regular group sittings in Boulder for the past several years. They also organize one-day courses from time to time. To mark Goenkaji's visit they had decided to hold a one-day course. Due to the limited capacity of the meditation venue, registration for the course was closed far in advance.

Since he had a busy morning schedule, Goenkaji decided to visit the one-day course site only to answer questions from meditators on the course.

On the way to the course site Mataji suggested that if Goenkaji took his lunch a little later he would be able to stay on to give Vipassana instructions after the question-and-answer session. Goenkaji's assistants were hesitant to allow this, but the issue was settled when Goenkaji agreed with Mataji saying—*sabba dānaṃ, dhamma dānaṃ jīnati*—the gift of Dhamma surpasses all other gifts. As far as time and health permits, he wants to teach Anapana or Vipassana whenever he gets the opportunity. And so he stayed on to give the gift of Vipassana to the lucky one-day course students.

A large number of long-time students were on the course. Some had learned Vipassana directly from Goenakji more than 20 years earlier. During the question period, one woman narrated how she had suffered from depression for many years and how Vipassana had helped her to relieve the condition almost completely. Goenkaji urged her to keep working at the level of sensations with the understanding that both the sensations and the depression are impermanent.

Another student asked whether the Pāli word *vedanā* meant physical sensations or mental feelings. In his answer, Goenkaji emphasized that physical sensations are crucial in the practice of Vipassana. Although sensations arise on the material body, the experience of them is a mental phenomenon. However, translating *vedanā* as feeling can be misleading, because people may take it to mean thoughts and emotions. In the Buddha's teaching, *vedanā* refers chiefly to the experience of physical sensations on the body. Observing real, physical, tangible sensations allows us to maintain a clear hold on reality.

Another student wanted to know whether to observe sensations only on the surface of the body, or to try and feel sensations inside the body too. Goenkaji's advice was to continue to work with sensations on the surface unless one is naturally aware of sensations inside the body. Unless there are uniform subtle sensations throughout the body one should not try to penetrate inside the body to look for sensations.

Someone else was curious to know how constant awareness of sensations can eradicate *saṅkhāras* (mental conditioning)? Goenkaji likened this process to a fire that consumes fuel to keep burning. As long as fuel is fed to the fire, the burning continues and the stock of fuel is liable to increase. If no fuel is given to the fire, however, the fire can sustain itself only by burning up the old fuel. It is the fuel of *saṅkhāras* that keeps the flow of life, or stream of consciousness in motion. If there is ignorance, each moment the mind generates a new *saṅkhāra* in reaction to sensations. But with the wisdom of Vipassana, the mind simply observes sensations with equanimity—no reaction, therefore no new *saṅkhāras*. As soon as one stops making new *saṅkhāras*, the stream of consciousness starts using up all the accumulated *saṅkhāras* of the past. This is how the mind gets purified to the depth.

One meditator commented that there is an apparent contradiction between "effort" and "effortless observation." Goenkaji explained that it is important to make effort on the path of Dhamma, but without generating any tension. A meditator should keep checking oneself to make sure one is not getting tense. In the beginning often meditators tend to generate tension out of their desire to work hard. But with time and practice, they slowly learn to maintain constant awareness and alertness with a relaxed mind. In Vipassana effort is needed to maintain awareness and equanimity but there should be no effort to create or change sensations. Thus it is an effortless effort.

Many people practice yoga and Vipassana. Goenkaji was asked which of the two should be practiced first in a daily routine. It was a matter of choice, he said, as yoga and Vipassana are compatible, even complementary. However, Goenkaji advised the students not to mix any meditational aspects of yoga with Vipassana. In response to a related question, he said that *mantras* should not be used with the practice of *pranayama*.

As often happens, some students walked up to Goenkaji to express gratitude to him. His usual reply is, "Thank Dhamma." Sometimes he adds, "Thank yourself for taking the time to practice and for making effort on the path of Dhamma. But don't develop ego, 'Look **I** worked so hard and **I** have progressed so much on the path.'"

After the question-and-answer session, Goenkaji gave Vipassana instructions to the group.

Day 47, May 26, Boulder, Colorado / Manhattan, New York
New York: The Sāvatthi of the Modern Age

Mataji packed the bags for another trip to New York, making sure Goenkaji had everything needed for this important visit—books, medications, suitable clothes, toiletries and various other items. It took eight hours for Goenkaji and Mataji to reach Manhattan from their motor home in Boulder! There was a drive of one and a half hours to Denver airport, a protracted wait for airport security procedures, a four-hour flight to New York and, finally, a one-hour drive to reach the apartment where they would be staying. This was the first time on the tour that Goenkaji had left the motor home for an overnight stay elsewhere.

At the time of the Buddha, the most populous city of India was Sāvatthi, which was the capital of the mighty Kosalan empire and also the largest commercial center in the land. As the financial capital of the world and headquarters of the United Nations, New York can be regarded as the Sāvatthi of today's world. This great city, which has freely taken into its fold people from all over the world, remained badly scarred by the terrorist attack of September 11, 2001.

In view of the city's importance, it seemed only fitting that Goenkaji was now making his third visit to New York since the tour began—this time to speak at the official *Vesākha* celebrations at the United Nations.

Day 48, May 27, Manhattan, New York
A Day of Recuperation

This was one of those rare days of the tour on which Goenkaji had no public engagements.

Goenkaji spent his time seeing various people and meeting with some of his assistant teachers and old students, to give guidance on administrative matters. He also used the available time to attend to correspondence with Vipassana centers and teachers from all over the world.

Happily, he was able to take a walk both in the morning and evening—something that is often impossible with his busy tour schedule. Goenkaji took walks in Central Park, which was within walking distance of the apartment where he was staying.

Day 49, May 28, United Nations, New York
The Buddha: A Super-Scientist of Peace

Goenkaji delivered the keynote address at the Celebration of the International Recognition of the *Vesākha*, at the United Nations, an annual event to honor the birth, enlightenment and final passing away of the Buddha. This year the event was being hosted by the Permanent Mission of the Union of Myanmar to the United Nations. The Ambassadors of the Permanent Missions of Sri Lanka, Cambodia and Myanmar each spoke briefly before Goenkaji's speech.

The talk, entitled "Buddha, the Super-Scientist of Peace," was given at the Dag Hammerskold Library Auditorium to an audience of Ambassadors, other United Nations dignitaries and associates, Buddhist monks and a few Vipassana meditators. Goenkaji put the teaching of the historical Buddha into a modern perspective.

> The world is afflicted with the malady of hatred, anxiety and fear. It needs a remedy from an extraordinary physician. The Buddha was just such an extraordinary physician—a great physician of peace and happiness. His teaching of peace and harmony is as relevant today as it was 26 centuries ago, when he set in motion the "wheel of Dhamma," the "wheel of

peace." If anything, it is even more relevant today. We have gathered here this afternoon to honor the teaching of this outstanding person in human history. Let us see how his teaching uproots the negative emotions that are at the root of cruel violence and how these can be changed into positive compassion. The negativity that produces so many atrocities results from blind beliefs and strong attachment to particular views.

For peace in a society, there has to be peace within individuals. There has to be peace within before there can be peace in the outside world.

Goenkaji explained how the Buddha had discovered the root cause of misery and the way out of it.

When one is working with sensations, one is working at the depth of mind. Whatever arises in the mind is accompanied by sensations on the body—*vedanāsamosaraṇā sabbe dhamma*. When even a thought arises in the mind, it is accompanied by a sensation on the body—*vedanāsamosaraṇā saṅkappavitakka*. This was one of the great discoveries of the Buddha... Another great discovery of the Buddha was that we generate *taṇhā* (craving) in response to *vedanā* (sensations)...

...When one observes sensations objectively, one starts coming out of ignorance. By understanding the impermanent nature of sensations, one generates *paññā* (wisdom) in response to *vedanā*. This is the law of nature. The law behind the natural order of phenomena is *Dhamma niyāmatā*. Buddha or no Buddha, *Dhamma niyāmatā* remains. The law is eternal. This is the bold declaration of a supreme scientist... just as the law of gravity remains true whether there is a Newton or not. Newton merely discovered the law and explained it to the world... Buddha said, "I have experienced this Law of Nature, the Law of Dependent Origination, within myself; and having experienced and understood it I declare it, teach it, clarify it, establish it and show it to others. Only after having seen it for myself do I declare it."

The entire audience responded to the talk with sincere respect and appreciation. Afterwards, at a reception, held at the United Nations Penthouse, many diplomats came to meet Goenkaji. They were enthusiastic in expressing their agreement with his address. Many of them had heard about Vipassana from friends and relatives. One ambassador revealed that his wife was a keen Vipassana meditator. When he read the programme just before the event he was pleasantly surprised to see Goenkaji listed as the keynote speaker. Unfortunately, since he had not been aware that Goenkaji was to speak at the *Vesākha* celebration, he had not mentioned the event to her. He joked that he would have to face his wife's displeasure for not having informed her. He even told Goenkaji that he would soon take a ten-day course for himself. The Indian Ambassador (of the Permanent Mission of India to the United Nations) also came to greet Goenkaji.

It was late when Goenkaji returned to the apartment. He was tired but satisfied that there were signs that the world was taking heed of the Buddha's eternal teaching.

Day 50, May 29, New York / San Diego, California
Coast to Coast
Early the next day Goenkaji flew from New York to San Diego.

While Goenkaji and Mataji were in New York, the tireless Dhamma caravan crew drove the motor homes from Boulder, Colorado to San Diego. They reached San Diego just in time for Goenkaji's arrival at the motor home park. The crew had to drive for long hours to make sure that they would reach San Diego before Goenkaji did.

In the evening, Goenkaji met for discussions with the teachers responsible for the spread of Vipassana in the People's Republic of China (Mainland China).

Day 51, May 30, San Diego, California
Visit to a Laboratory

Goenkaji often says that meditators must work in the laboratory of their own body and mind. They must work within the corporeal structure to understand the interaction of mind and matter—how mind influences matter and how matter influences mind.

While in San Diego, Goenkaji went to a conventional laboratory. He visited a pathology lab to have his blood sugar level checked, to ensure that his personal glucometer was giving correct readings.

Later that same morning, he talked to the producer of a National Public Radio show to discuss the interview that they planned to air later.

In the evening, he gave a public talk in the Montezuma Hall at San Diego State University. He stressed that people who have migrated to the U.S. should be loyal to their adopted land, ensuring their actions are in no way harmful to the people of this country. To a question as to why Buddhism was driven out of India, Goenkaji replied, "Because it became Buddhism!" Although a few people may use the word "Buddhism" to mean the Buddha's teaching, without any sectarian connotation, for the majority of people the term "Buddhism" signifies an organized religion. Goenkaji explains how India forgot Buddha because his practical teaching of Vipassana was corrupted and ultimately lost.

Day 52, May 31, Orange County, California
Questions

The Dhamma caravan left San Diego in the morning to travel to Irvine, where Goenkaji led the Vipassana session on a one-day course held at a Mormon Church. He also made time to answer questions from the course participants.

One meditator asked about the role of prayer in Vipassana. Goenkaji replied that praying to get something from an invisible being merely increases one's dependence on others. On the other hand, if one practices Dhamma properly, whatever benevolent invisible beings there are will certainly be pleased. The important thing, therefore, is to walk on the path of Dhamma.

Another student wanted to know about advanced stages and attainments in meditation. Goenkaji replied that the main yardstick of progress on the path of Dhamma is whether your life is improving for the better—whether you are living a more peaceful and happy life.

In response to a question about *Kundalini*, Goenkaji explained that after the Buddha's practical teaching was lost in India, mere discussions about the experiences that arise from Vipassana remained. Thus, new practices were started in an effort to produce such experiences, but these attempts could enable people to feel sensations only at certain points along the spinal cord, called *chakras*, which are particularly sensitive. There was no understanding of the impermanent nature of these sensations and no effort to maintain equanimity. Rather than enabling the eradication of mental conditioning (*saṅkhāras*), such practices only reinforced the habit pattern of craving.

Another meditator was apprehensive about the mental effects of serving extremely sick people for a long time. Goenkaji told him that serving sick people is a part of Dhamma. It strengthens one's practice. As long as there is base of compassion and loving-kindness such service yields immense strength.

When an old student approached Goenkaji to say, "Thank you for your teaching," she was quickly corrected. "Not my teaching. It is the Buddha's teaching."

Siddhartha's Quest

In the evening, Goenkaji returned to the same venue to give a public talk, which was simultaneously translated into Chinese. Goenkaji told the story of the Buddha's life from the time he set out for enlightenment. After leaving home in search of a way out of the inherent suffering of existence, Siddhartha learned various absorption meditations (*samādhis*). All these practices, which work by concentrating the mind on some particular object, give the mind a deep tranquillity and also certain amount of purity. The ascetic prince found, however, that despite having attained the very highest levels of absorption (*samādhis*), he remained unable to remove the deep-seated mental impurities.

So the *bodhisatta* (bodhisattva) then turned to the practice of austerities and fasting, out of the commonly held belief that torturing the body purifies the mind. Over time, his body became little more than a skeleton. He found that this extreme self-mortification could not help him to attain further mental purification. Thus, six years after commencing his quest he gave up the practice of austerities. It was only at this point, after having renounced the two extremes of sensual indulgence and self-mortification, that he made his groundbreaking discovery of Vipassana—the practice that enabled him to purify the totality of the mind—and thereby attained full enlightenment.

We are all very fortunate that this path of Vipassana is still available today in all its efficacy. For this, we owe thanks to the land of Myanmar (Burma), where the practice was preserved in its pristine purity through the millennia. Using this simple technique, people everywhere can liberate themselves from the bondage of mental impurities.

After the public talk, the tour caravan traveled to the Myanmar monastery in Azusa, reaching there at about midnight.

Day 53, June 1, Azusa, California
Myanmar Monastery

The volunteers in the Dhamma caravan felt very much at home in the Myanmar monastery. The monks were extremely hospitable. The Myanmar lay people who supported the monastery were also very helpful.

Goenkaji paid respect to the Sangha during his morning walk.

In the evening, he gave a public talk in Los Angeles, at the Wadsworth Theater in Brentwood. He explained how Vipassana is an art of living a happy and peaceful life—a life that is good for oneself and good for others. The lively talk had people laughing in the beginning. Later, as Goenkaji explained how Vipassana is a science of the interaction of mind and matter, the audience became serious and listened in rapt attention. Then, as happens at most talks, the mood lightened again during the question-and-answer session.

One person wanted to know the place of sex in married life. Goenkaji replied that physical relations with a single partner does not break the five precepts and is not harmful. However, if one goes on changing partners to seek out more and more sensual pleasure, one becomes engulfed by the fire of lust, resulting in constant agitation and misery.

Someone asked, "If I don't react then how can I have any fun in life?" Amid laughter from the audience Goenkaji replied that it is all right to have fun in life. "But make sure that you *really* are enjoying life," he warned. "For this it is important that you have no attachment to your enjoyment—that you don't become miserable when it comes to an end."

Day 54, June 2, Azusa, California
Sangha Dana

The expatriate communities of a number of South Asian countries came together to organize a *Sangha Dāna* on behalf of Goenkaji and Mataji. It was a massive undertaking to bring together monks and nuns from different traditions. This auspicious event was made possible because of the tireless efforts of U Tin Htoon, with help from Henry Kao and many other selfless volunteers.

On the day of the *Sangha Dāna*, the venue was filled with more than a thousand people. Goenkaji and Mataji offered food and requisites to the Sangha.

In his introductory speech, Ven. Piyananda, the president of the Southern California Buddhist Council, told the audience that he had taken his first ten-day course with Goenkaji in 1973. Later on, Goenkaji gave a Dhamma talk.

It is a great joy to see and pay respect to monks from various traditions—a rainbow spectrum. These are all branches of the same tree—they all get nutrition from the Buddha Dhamma, the essence of which is *paṭicca-samuppāda* (Dependent Origination), the Four Noble Truths and the Eightfold Noble Path, which are accepted by all as the basic, principal teaching of the Buddha. These are acceptable not only to Buddhists but to all people of all faiths.

Morality, concentration of mind and purity of mind is common to all faiths, all religions.

For morality, one-pointed concentration of a wholesome mind—*kusala cittassa ekaggatā*—is necessary, which means the mind should be free from craving and aversion. The Buddha gave a simple technique, where one concentrates one's mind on the in-breath and out-breath, keeping one's attention at the tip of the nose (*nāsikagge*) or just below the nostrils above the upper lip (*uttaraoṭṭhassa vemajjhappadese*). When one practices this way, the mind becomes sharp enough to start feeling sensations in this area. As a meditator starts observing the realities within, he discovers the same realities that the Buddha discovered.

The special discovery of the Buddha was a chain of cause and effect relationships. *Imasmiṃ sati idaṃ hoti, imasmiṃ asati idaṃ na hoti*. If this (cause) is present then that (result) comes; if this (cause) is not present then that (result) does not come.

In dependent origination, the Buddha explains, *saḷāyatana paccayā phassa, phassa paccayā vedanā, vedanā paccayā taṇhā*—dependent on the six sense doors contact arises, dependent on contact sensations arise, and dependent on sensations craving and aversion arise.

Goenkaji also talked about how there is a revival of interest in the Buddha's teaching in India.

In the evening, he met with Mr. Robert Hover and his wife, who had come to Myanmar Monastery in Azusa to see Goenkaji. Mr. Hover was one of the earliest western students of Sayagyi U Ba Khin. Goenkaji was very happy to see his old friend and talked with him for a long time.

Day 55, June 3, Azusa, California / Dhamma Mahāvana, North Fork, California

Khanti (Tolerance)

It was a very busy morning. Goenkaji had to leave the monastery early in the morning to meet Ven. Daw Dhammethi at another monastery. She had hosted the first Vipassana courses that Goenkaji taught when he returned to Myanmar in 1990 after an absence of 20 years from his motherland. The meeting was interrupted for a telephone interview that was aired live on National Public Radio in Philadelphia.

Goenkaji returned to the monastery where the motor homes were parked and was greeted by a reporter and staff photographer from the Los Angeles Times. The reporter, Ms. Hilary McGregor, interviewed Goenkaji in his motor home for an hour as he traveled to the Museum of Tolerance in Los Angeles. (Her article "Driven to Enlighten" appeared in the LA Times two days later, on June 5.)

Goenkaji visited the Museum of Tolerance not only because he has worked tirelessly for many years to teach tolerance, but also because he wanted to see for himself how museums are utilizing modern technology for educational purposes. The exhibition gallery at the Global Pagoda that is now being constructed in Mumbai, will serve to educate millions of visitors per year about the uplifting truth of the Buddha and his teaching. Although Goenkaji, Mataji and the other meditators accompanying him had known of the gruesome nature of the holocaust, at the museum they were deeply moved again to know in more details the immensity of this man-made tragedy.

Tolerance is one of the ten *pāramis* (virtues) that need to be cultivated in order to attain the ultimate spiritual goal of full liberation.

Tolerance is essential for maintaining peace in human society—tolerance of different ethnicities, cultures, languages, faiths; tolerance of the actions of others; and tolerance of views that are different to one's own. When there is purity, love and compassion in the mind tolerance develops naturally.

From the Museum of Tolerance the Dhamma caravan departed for the California Vipassana Center, *Dhamma Mahāvana*, near North Fork, arriving just before midnight.

Day 56, June 4, Dhamma Mahāvana, North Fork, California
Dhamma Mahāvana

Dhamma Mahāvana was now the second center to host the Dhamma caravan on the tour. Goenkaji's motor home was parked on the *shānti pathār* (peace plateau). That evening, Goenkaji gave a public talk in the nearby city of Fresno.

We all face misery in different forms. There is the misery of disease, old age and death; the misery of losing near and dear ones in wars and natural calamities, as well as the psychological trauma of survivors, which is so difficult to heal; the misery of feeling anxiety about the threats to one's own safety and the safety of loved ones. We are all concerned about the senseless killings occurring in different parts of the world. Innocent men, women and children are being killed—not because of any personal enmity but merely because they belong to a particular religious denomination or ethnic community.

Is there a way out of this suffering? Certainly! In a world afflicted by terrorism and war on the one hand, and the rampant escapism of sensual entertainments on the other, Vipassana helps one to find peace within oneself.

Day 57, June 5, Dhamma Mahāvana, North Fork, California
Like a Mother Hen Looking After Her Chicks

During Goenkaji's extensive travels, whenever he spends time at a Vipassana center, he meets with the trust members, inquires about current projects and offers guidance to Dhamma workers in their meditation practice. As a Dhamma teacher, he looks after his disciples with all the care of a mother hen tending to her chicks.

Today was an opportunity for Goenkaji to check and provide guidance on major development projects being undertaken at the California Vipassana Center, *Dhamma Mahāvana*. The center trust reported on the rapid strides it was taking in the spread of Dhamma. Goenkaji met with the trust as a group and also met individually with Dhamma workers. Among those who met him were two long-serving meditators battling with terminal illnesses, meditators facing family or financial difficulties, as well as many others enjoying good health and prosperity. All of these servants of Dhamma—whether seeking advice about serious problems or coming just to pay respect—talked to Goenkaji of how Vipassana had helped them to remain calm and brave through the thick and thin of life. All of them were smiling.

Goenkaji went to the beautiful meditation hall to answer questions from the students on the three-day old students' course that was in progress. One student asked how she could differentiate between determination and attachment. Goenkaji urged her to work with a strong determination whenever she was doing something that was good for her and good for society. "But if you fail, smile! If you get upset when you fail in your determination, then it means that you are attached to it."

Be Like a Lotus

Another student asked Goenkaji how she could remain unaffected by the immoral climate of western society, and its endless distractions. Goenkaji replied, "Like a lotus flower that blooms in all its beauty and glory without allowing the muddy water in which it grows to stick to it."

Day 58, June 6, Dhamma Mahāvana, North Fork / Saratoga Springs Campground, Saratoga, California

Saratoga Springs

Though the crew of the caravan would have liked to stay at the center longer, they had to leave for Saratoga, the next stop on the tour itinerary. Since Goenkaji's volition is always to spread Dhamma as widely as possible, he often agrees to quite grueling travel schedules.

Before leaving the center, Goenkaji met a few old students.

The caravan crew ate lunch on the road and reached their next campground by evening.

Day 59, June 7, Saratoga Springs Campground / Cupertino, California

Peace Amid Chaos

By mid-morning, a huge crowd of about 300 children and teenagers descended upon the campground where the caravan was staying. The sounds of loud music, screaming children and blaring microphone announcements filled the air throughout the day. Despite the cacophony, the small area where the caravan was parked remained an oasis of peace.

Weekend Spirituality

In the evening, Goenkaji gave a public talk at the Flint Theater at De Anza College in Cupertino. A lively question-and-answer session followed the talk.

Two questions that Goenkaji is frequently asked are: "Why don't you offer shorter meditation courses?" and "Why don't you charge money like other meditation teachers do?"

Goenkaji explained, "Dhamma is priceless. The moment you attach a price tag to it, it gets devalued." The Buddha said, *dhammena na vaṇiṃ care*—do not make a business of Dhamma.

In business the customer is always right. Since some people would like shorter courses, some teachers may decide to arrange and teach short courses without any regard for the proper atmosphere and training that a beginner needs. In such courses, people would only be dabbling at the surface of the mind. Although there would certainly be some benefits, three days is not enough for a student to learn to observe the reality at the depth of the mind. Goenkaji pointed out that in the past he had tried offering short 3-day courses of Anapana but found that they did not really benefit people.

Continuity of practice for an extended period is essential in Vipassana. Short courses simply don't offer that opportunity.

Furthermore, there is a risk that people may become complacent if they get some benefit from such a course, because they may think that they have understood the whole technique—that there is no need to go any further. In view of this, taking a shorter course could actually be a hurdle to reaching the root of the mind where impurities arise and multiply.

There are also some who may be put off from experiencing Vipassana after doing a short course, thinking, "Is that all there is to the technique?"

I want people to really benefit. I want them to come out of all their misery. Therefore, the course has to be long enough to really get to the depth of the mind. Traditionally, until about a century ago, Vipassana was taught in six-week retreats, but in modern times the courses were shortened. When the duration was reduced to ten days it was found that people still got an outline of the technique, but that if it was reduced further most didn't even get an outline. I don't want people to waste their time. Human life is so invaluable.

Happiness is a serious matter. We spend years and years in school and college studying things that often have little relevance to our lives, yet we are so reluctant to spare even 10 days to look at ourselves and learn to live a happy and harmonious life.

A man in his twenties asked whether it was not more important at his age to focus on achieving success in his career, getting married, etc. than on striving for the experience of *nirvāṇa (nibbāna)*? Goenkaji explained that *vāṇa (bāna)* means fire, so that *nirvāṇa* means the total extinction of the fire of mental impurities, whose burning keeps us continually miserable. Goenkaji asked, "Why do you want to burn?" He then added that with less fire, both one's career and family life will be more successful and more peaceful!

Despite the fact that Goenkaji is constantly stressing that Vipassana does not make people inactive, many remain afraid that if they take up the meditation practice they will lose their drive and ambition. Goenkaji explained that as well as giving peace and happiness, Vipassana also makes people active and dynamic.

Another question was, "Are the gods (*devas*) real?" Goenkaji replied, "Of course they are real. Anyone can become a god. You can become a god if you acquire the divine qualities of selfless love, compassion, sympathetic joy and equanimity."

Day 60, June 8, Saratoga Springs Campground / Berkeley / Anthony Chabot Regional Park, Oakland, California

Silicon Valley Professionals

In the morning, Goenkaji went to the campus of Hewlett Packard to give a talk sponsored by the Silicon Valley Indian Professionals Association. The capacity audience consisted largely of young computer professionals from Silicon Valley.

Mental Pollution in the Office

Mental balance and mental cultivation are important for every section of society, but especially so for business people. When one is successful from a worldly point of view—that is, when one has a lot of money and fame—one tends to become ego-centered. This in turn makes one short-tempered. One cannot tolerate anything that goes against one's wishes. Such a businessman remains angry and makes the atmosphere at the office very tense. The employees work out of fear and often their talent is not fully utilized. This was what was happening to me and my staff before I started practicing Vipassana.

When it was suggested that I join a Vipassana course, I faced two big barriers:

Firstly, thinking that this practice was Buddhism, I remembered the Indian saying, *swadharme nidhanam shreyam, paradharmo bhayāvaho*—"It is better to die in one's own religion than to go to any other religion." But after my teacher, Sayagyi U Ba Khin, compassionately explained that Vipassana is nothing but *sīla*, *samādhi* and *paññā* [morality, mental concentration and wisdom], I was reassured. In fact, I was already giving many discourses on the Bhagavad Gita ideal of *sthitaprajña* (being established in wisdom), yet I was unable to realize it for myself. I would tearfully recite prayers to request more wisdom. For some time, my devotional fervor would give me a relatively calm mind. But then again the old habit pattern of anger and ego would dominate me. I started seriously searching for something that would take me to the ideal of *sthitaprajña*.

Secondly, I was a very busy person and found it difficult to spare ten days of my life to learn this technique.

When I started practicing Vipassana I learned how we make the atmosphere around us tense by generating defilements in the mind. This is mental pollution. Once the mind starts getting purer, the interaction with employees and colleagues changes. There is genuine warmth and goodwill.

If there is mental pollution in the office atmosphere, then one burns oneself and burns others—the creative ability of the employees is stunted; the productive energy is wasted due to negative emotions.

Goenkaji asked the young professionals to be really selfish. To be really selfish one must look after one's own peace and happiness. When one is peaceful, people around become peaceful and happy. Then one finds that one's peace and happiness helps one's business career as well.

Vipassana results in a sharper mind, making one more adept at solving technical and administrative problems.

There were many questions from the young computer professionals, some of whom were hearing about this simple, logical and scientific teaching of ancient India for the first time. They asked questions about the impact of Buddha's teaching on India and how India lost it, and about how it compared with other meditation techniques they had heard about. Meeting Goenkaji at the end of the talk, a good number of the young professionals promised to give a trial to the practical teaching of the Buddha.

Not Merely to Satisfy Curiosity

That same evening, Goenkaji gave a public talk at the Berkeley campus of the University of California. Berkeley is renowned for its vibrant and active student community and student activism. Goenkaji had given public talks here before—more than ten years earlier. A large number of people gathered to hear him speak today.

Vipassana is a process of exploring the truth within, exploring the mind-matter phenomenon. But it is not merely to satisfy one's intellectual curiosity. Last century, a Berkeley scientist made a big contribution to the understanding that everything in the material world is mere wavelets, mere vibrations, that there is no solidity in it at all. The Buddha proclaimed this same truth more than 2500 years ago. The difference is that the Buddha discovered this truth without any scientific instruments, when he explored the reality within to find a way out of all suffering. Vipassana is that path out of all suffering. It is self-realization through self-observation. It is the experiential understanding of how one generates misery and how one can come out that habit.

If one has craving for a pleasant experience, there will be inherent aversion to unpleasant experiences. If one has aversion to an unpleasant experience, there will be inherent craving for pleasant experiences.

Mind-washing

Later on he answered questions from the audience and gave private interviews. One person asked, "Is this brainwashing?" Goenkaji replied, "No. It is mind-washing. It purifies your mind and makes you happy and peaceful. Don't get brain-washed! Believe your own experience. And keep working on purifying your mind to live a better life."

After the talk, as Goenkaji and others drove to the beautiful Anthony Chabot Regional Park in the mountains, a few wild deer and other animals crossed their path. It was quite late and everyone was tired. They had to start early the next day to go to the Jain Temple in Milpitas where Goenkaji was scheduled to give a public talk in Hindi.

Day 61, June 9, Oakland / Jain Temple, Milpitas / Hayward / Petaluma, CA

Vīra and Mahavīra: A Warrior and a Great Warrior

The hall at the Jain temple was full of Indian expatriates. Some of them had heard Goenkaji's talks before, but only in English, so they were looking forward to hearing him speak in Hindi.

Dharma (*Dhamma* in Pāli) is the "nature of things." It also means the "law of nature," which when followed makes one happy and peaceful, and helps one to generate nothing but love and compassion for others.

All vocal and physical violence starts with violence in the mind. The nature of violence is that whenever the mind generates violence one becomes agitated and distressed. The nature of non-violence is that whenever the mind generates non-violence, one experiences immense peace and happiness.

This requires hard work. One has to work hard to liberate oneself from the bondage of defilements that time and again makes the mind violent. One who liberates oneself from the bondage of defilements is a *vīra*. And one who liberates oneself and also helps others to become liberated from the bondage of defilements is called a *mahavīra*.

Walk the talk

The discourse lasted more than an hour and there were many questions from the audience. To questions about philosophical beliefs in India, Goenkaji remarked, "Everyone in India is a philosopher but what is the use of all these philosophies if one's life doesn't reflect one's talk?" He also clarified how various misconceptions about the Buddha have harmed Indians.

Intellectually, we all believe that our physical bodies are impermanent (*nashvar sharir*), but in actual fact there is so much attachment to the body that we have come to regard it as "I." This is *dehātma buddhi*. Similarly, although we can readily agree that mind is impermanent, we still have a great deal of attachment to it. This is *cittātma buddhi*. Without understanding what the Buddha really taught, Indians have maligned his teaching and stayed away from it, protesting that he doesn't believe in Soul, or that he doesn't believe in God.

Another misconception in the minds of many Indians is that the Buddha was *nāstika*. Goenakji has explained that *nāstika* originally meant one who does not believe in karma and its fruit. When one looks within with Vipassana, one can see for oneself how one creates karma.

For centuries people have been afraid of the Buddha's teaching. Now they are discovering that it is not something to fear, but rather something that helps in overcoming fear; something that makes one fearless.

Despite the fact that this wonderful technique originated in India and made India a world teacher in the field of spirituality, many Indians are reluctant to try it. Goenkaji understands this unfortunate fact well, from his own resistance to the Buddha's teaching over 50 years ago, and also from the resistance of many Indians he encountered when he started teaching Vipassana in India 33 years ago.

From Milpitas, Goenkaji traveled to Hayward where about 400 meditators had gathered for a one-day course. One student wanted to know about the milestones along the path of meditation. Goenkaji explained that the one should give importance only to the present moment. "Equanimity is the only yardstick to measure one's progress on the path of Dhamma." Another student who complained of poor concentration was advised by Goenkaji to practice more Anapana. One meditator was worried about her livelihood. She said that while she doesn't directly do anything wrong in her job, the company she works for is involved in certain practices that are not completely wholesome. Goenkaji answered that that if one is not involved personally in any unwholesome practices then one should not worry—there is no reason to feel guilty about something over which one has no control.

Whilst almost everyone who takes a ten-day course benefits to some degree and agrees that Vipassana is helpful, it is difficult for people to keep up daily meditation practice at home after a course. Yet, without continued daily meditation, ideally in the morning and evening, one cannot get the optimum benefit of Vipassana. This is why one-day courses and group sittings are very important. They help meditators to "charge their batteries," to give them renewed strength and inspiration to maintain their daily practice.

The Dhamma caravan drove from Milpitas to Petaluma. The campground was close to the venues for the one-day course and public talks scheduled for the following day.

Day 62, June 10, Santa Rosa, CA
Suffering Defined
In the morning, Goenkaji led the Anapana session at a one-day course at Sonoma State University. In the evening, he returned to the university to give a public talk.

As the hall was filling to capacity and people continued to stream in, many Vipassana meditators kindly gave up their places in the hall to give others an opportunity to listen to Goenkaji in person, and, hopefully, get inspired to take a ten-day course. This same practice was followed at all the public talk venues on the tour. In this case, the old students congregated in the lobby, where the discourse was relayed on a closed-circuit TV.

The Buddha's teaching is as relevant today as in the past—because there is as much misery today as there was in the past; because human beings generate misery the same way today as they did in ancient times. We all suffer. Life starts with crying. Once born, one is bound to encounter the sufferings of sickness and old age.

Throughout life, one encounters things that one does not like, and is separated from things that one likes. Unwanted things happen, wanted things do not happen, and one feels miserable. Even the most powerful person on the earth cannot ensure that only wanted things will happen or that unwanted things won't happen in life.

The Buddha went to the root of this problem, and discovered the solution for liberation from all misery. He realized that we keep reacting to the pleasant and unpleasant sensations we feel on the body with craving and aversion. And due to these mental impurities or habit patterns, we remain agitated and miserable.

Reciting or chanting a word or mantra can help calm the mind, but only for some time, and only at the surface of the mind. But by doing this, one is not facing the impurity that has arisen. If one keeps on repeating a word or a mantra, one becomes enveloped by the vibrations of that word or mantra, while deep inside the habit pattern of craving and aversion continues unabated. It is like singing a lullaby to put a baby to sleep. Thus, this is not a lasting solution to the problem.

One might recite the name of a god or a goddess in the belief that he or she will be pleased with the recitation. One doesn't understand that if that god or goddess has really created the laws of nature, he or she would be more pleased if one obeyed those laws! The law of nature is such that if one defiles one's mind with any impurity such as anger, hatred, lust, or jealousy, one becomes unhappy then and there. On the other hand, if one purifies the mind, maintains equanimity, or generates love and compassion, one remains happy and peaceful.

In the beginning of my first course, I expected to be taught the recitation of the Buddha's name. When that didn't happen, I thought, 'What is the use of watching the breath and watching the sensations?' Soon it became clear to me—as it becomes clear to all Vipassana meditators—that breath and sensations are closely related to the mind and mental impurities. One starts understanding the law of nature and seeing how one keeps generating misery for oneself and spreading this misery all around.

From Cruelty to Compassion

As usual, there were questions from the audience about terror and terrorism and how Vipassana can help with that. Goenkaji recounted the story of Aṅgulimāla from the time of Buddha. Without any weapons of mass destruction, this terrorist had killed 999 human beings. His cruelty and inhumanity was highlighted by the fact that he wore a garland made of the fingers of his victims, hence his name (*aṅgulimāla* means "garland of fingers"). Then, just as he was seeking out his one thousandth victim, he came across the Buddha, after which he was totally transformed—not by mere preaching, but through this same practice of Vipassana. Working seriously, he eventually became an *arahat*—a fully purified and perfectly saintly person. When this same Aṅgulimāla, now a monk, walked for alms through towns and villages, he was occasionally stoned and beaten with sticks when people recognized him as the killer of a friend or relative. But even as blood oozed from the wounds on his body, only love and compassion flowed from his mind.

It was not only Aṅgulimāla who was converted in this way. So many contract killers and murderers—both at the time of the Buddha and after the Buddha—renounced their violent ways. Today Vipassana is bringing similar results to criminals in the prisons of India, the U.S., Spain and many other countries.

Goenkaji, Start a Vipassana Center Here!

A member of the audience called on Goenkaji to start a Vipassana center in Santa Rosa. Goenkaji laughed and said, "I don't start centers. The meditators do." It is the local meditators who start a center in any area. Usually the first step in this direction is that the Vipassana meditators in an area come together regularly for weekly group sittings and one-day courses. They then start organizing ten-day courses under the guidance of an authorized assistant teacher. Once a few ten-day courses are held in an area and enough financial and human resources are gathered, the local meditators start looking for a suitable place to establish a permanent center. Guidelines for running non-center courses, establishing a trust or developing a center are available on a website for old students.

Since Santa Rosa has many Vipassana meditators and a wealth of enthusiasm for Dhamma, it is only a matter of time before a center arises here. The same is true for many other places around the world!

Day 63, June 11, Santa Rosa, CA / Albion, CA

Training Under Sayagyi U Ba Khin

In the morning, Goenkaji gave an interview to New Dimensions Radio. In the discussion he explained how he was attracted to Vipassana despite his staunch orthodox Hindu background and his initial prejudice against the teaching of the Buddha. From 1955 to 1969, he meditated under the close guidance of his teacher, Sayagyi U Ba Khin. This long and intimate training period has given him great strength throughout his mission of spreading Dhamma. Sayagyi would often say of Vipassana: "It is very easy and yet it is very difficult. It is very difficult and yet it is very easy." It is easy in the sense that it is simple to follow and practice. But it is difficult because our mind is constantly distracted by so many negativities. That is why determination is so essential for continuing on the path of Dhamma.

Sayagyi authorized Goenkaji to teach Vipassana and entrusted him with the task of taking Vipassana back to its homeland and, from there, spreading it all over the world.

Aware Outside, Aware Inside

Talking about the benefits of a ten-day course, Goenkaji explains that although a holiday at the beach or at a resort can leave one feeling rejuvenated, this feeling lasts only as long as one is distracted from the problems of life. On returning home, as one is gradually exposed to the same tensions and strains, one continues to react to them in the same harmful manner as before—because one does not know how to deal with them. Vipassana offers a tool for dealing with all the daily ups and downs of life. With Vipassana, one can be fully attentive to the worldly realities outside and simultaneously remain aware of one's own mental state.

Today's world offers a vast assortment of sensual diversions and entertainments. People have come to equate these fleeting pleasures with happiness and pursue them with ever greater craving. And the greater the attachment to such pleasant experiences, the greater the fear and insecurity about losing them. As the Buddha said, *kāmato jāyatī soko, kāmato jāyatī bhayaṃ*—"from craving arises grief, from craving arises fear." The diverse sensual entertainments available today have made people even more fearful.

Vipassana helps one to see by direct personal experience the fleeting nature of all worldly pleasures and how they inevitably lead to suffering, by experience—direct, personal experience. As long as one depends solely on the very limited faculty of intellect, it is impossible to properly understand Dhamma. Real wisdom can only be cultivated through direct realization of the truth. Only such wisdom can give true understanding and true happiness.

The interviewer asked, "When does this process of suffering start? At birth?" Goenkaji explained that a person is born anew at every moment. If one is ignorant of this, then each and every moment the mind generates a new impurity. Rather than going into the hypothetical question of when it all began, the important thing is to pay attention to the present moment of experience. The flow of consciousness continues from moment to moment, and at each moment one needs to be on guard to avoid generating a new *saṅkhāra* (mental conditioning).

Supernatural Powers

The interviewer wanted to know whether some of Goenkaji's students have developed supernatural powers. Goenkaji replied that supernatural powers can be harmful, because they give rise to ego and attachment to such special abilities. A meditator can easily forget that the real goal is mental purification. As long as the mind is contaminated by impurities such as anger, hatred, fear, ego, jealousy, lust and greed, one remains miserable, regardless of the special abilities one may have cultivated. So, what is the use of these supernatural powers?

When the interviewer brought up the September 11 terrorist attacks, Goenkaji said that people who commit acts of violence in the name of their religion do not really understand their religion. Goenkaji reminded the interviewer that *salaam walekum*, the customary greeting in most Islamic countries, means "may peace be with you."

After the interview, the Dhamma caravan set off for the next stop on the tour, Albion, on the Mendocino coast. Slowly, the vehicles snaked their way along the winding roads through the beautiful hills of Sonoma County into Mendocino. The slow vehicles of the caravan had to stop on the shoulder of the narrow single-lane road many times to allow faster vehicles to pass. After finally reaching the Pacific ocean, the caravan drove along the spectacular coast for some time and pulled in at a campsite on a small beach. Soon after, as a blanket of fog rolled in from the sea, it suddenly became extremely cold.

Before the invasion of fog, Goenkaji had left for a meeting nearby with local trust members, assistant teachers and other meditators. When he returned it was so cold and foggy that he was unable to take his evening walk.

Goenkaji had been in this area more than 20 years earlier to conduct non-center courses.

Day 64, June 12, Albion, CA / Fort Bragg, CA / Albion, CA
Eagles Hall

Goenkaji and Mataji took their morning walk in the beautiful gardens of an estate maintained by a meditator. Mataji was delighted to see huge sweet smelling roses of every hue.

In the evening, Goenkaji gave a talk at Eagles Hall in Fort Bragg, a very old wooden building that appeared rather stark and unwelcoming in the morning. By the time of the talk, however, local Vipassana students had meditated in the hall for an hour; chairs were put out for the audience; and the black Halloween decorations that nobody had bothered to take down from the stage were covered with some white, gold and light blue drapes. The only remaining problem was that Goenkaji needed to climb up high rickety steps to reach the stage. The problem was solved by placing small blocks of wood on the steps.

The atmosphere in the hall was further enriched by the arrival of a group of graceful monks and nuns from a nearby monastery, who were all respectfully escorted to the front row.

Vipassana is a journey within. In Vipassana one learns that peace of mind is lost the moment one starts to react to one's sensations with craving and aversion. When there is a lack of experience of the reality within then there is ignorance. There is no moment in life, in any posture and any position, when there is no sensation on the body. And as long as there is ignorance one keeps on reacting to these sensations with craving and aversion.

From Gross to Subtle

One starts the work of eradicating this habit of reaction by learning to concentrate the mind. The mind becomes sharp if the area it focuses on is small. To investigate the mind-matter phenomenon the mind needs to be sharp. The sharper the mind, the deeper it penetrates. However, as one starts observing the breath, the mind wanders away. One tends to get upset by this, but is told, "Just accept, 'my mind has wandered away,' and come back to the awareness of breath. Keep trying patiently and persistently." As the mind becomes calm, the breath becomes shorter and shorter. As the breath becomes shorter and shorter, the mind becomes subtler and subtler.

During the process of investigating the truth inside, one progresses from gross realities to subtler and subtler realities. This journey from gross to subtle leads one to experience all the ultimate realities. These four ultimate realities are: *rūpa* (matter), *citta* (mind/consciousness), *cetasika* (mental concomitants) and *nibbāna*.

After the talk, Goenkaji met with the monks and nuns. They expressed their pleasure at meeting Goenkaji and their gratitude for his teaching. One of the monks mentioned that his first experience of meditation (before he took robes) was with Goenkaji. After meeting with the monks and nuns, Goenkaji and Mataji met with others from the audience.

A young child rose to the stage and offered a flower to Mataji.

Day 65, June 13, Crescent City RV Park, California
Minor Accident, Major Delay
The Dhamma caravan's next destination was Ashland, Oregon. Since it was not possible to cover the distance to Ashland in one day, the caravan decided to make an overnight stop on the way, at a campground along the Pacific Coast. This decision proved prudent, as within half an hour or so of setting off, the rear tires of Goenkaji's motor home were punctured by sharp rocks by the road on a sharp bend. Luckily, the driver was able to maneuver the motor home into a large turnout, and the whole caravan was able to gather there to help. Some crew members made phone calls to try and locate new tires. Another made tea for everyone. Two experienced mechanics among the crew quickly changed a tire and extracted a piece of the muffler system, which had been damaged in the accident. As the motor home sat stranded on the roadside, Goenkaji continued his reading. A senior teacher accompanying the caravan in a car seized the opportunity to seek Goenkaji's guidance on various issues pertaining to Vipassana activities in his area.

After a delay of more than two hours the caravan continued on its way until it was met further along the road by the repair vehicle, which brought another tire.

Ancient Tree, Ancient Tradition
Along the way the caravan took a small detour so that Goenkaji and Mataji could experience an ancient "drive-thru tree." Since the motor home was too large to drive through the opening at the base of the tree, Goenkaji walked from the car

park to see the 2400 year-old chandelier tree. Lovingly, he touched the huge trunk of the tree—31 feet in diameter. It is remarkable to think that this tree must have sprouted around the time of Ashoka, the great Indian emperor responsible for spreading the message of Dhamma beyond the Indian subcontinent. It is thanks to his great foresight that the jewel of Dhamma is available to us today.

The caravan continued its journey through forests of redwood trees, which are amongst the most ancient trees on earth. The tall and benign-looking figures of the trees on either side of the road almost completely blocked out the sunlight. All in the caravan somehow felt a great affection for these trees.

When the caravan reached the Crescent City RV Park at 8 p.m., all were ready for bed.

Day 66, June 14, Glenyan Campground, Ashland, Oregon
To Warmer Climes

In the morning, a light, misty rain confined Goenkaji and Mataji to their motor home. The Dhamma caravan set out for Ashland, Oregon at around 11 a.m. For the last few days, the weather had been quite cold, with a biting wind. But now, as the caravan moved towards Oregon, it began to get warmer. There was bright sunshine for the better part of the day.

The caravan reached the Glenyan Campground in Ashland in the evening.

As always, the crew members who did not have a place to sleep in the motor homes pitched tents in the vicinity of the caravan vehicles. Despite the inconvenience they felt fortunate to be part of the tour—helping their teacher in his Dhamma mission. They all appreciated how difficult it was for Goenkaji to have undertaken the tour at such an advanced age.

Day 67, June 15, Ashland, Oregon
Within This Fathom-Long Body

Though Ashland is only a small town, it boasts a large number of Vipassana meditators, and many of them gathered for a one-day course at the Hidden Spring Wellness Center. Goenkaji joined the course to answer questions from the students.

In the evening, Goenkaji gave a public talk to a capacity crowd at the town's Unitarian Church.

The truth of suffering and the way out of suffering has to be realized within the framework of the body, within the mind-matter phenomenon. Within this fathom-long body one finds the source of misery and the way out of it.

Craving and aversion have become the deeply ingrained habit pattern of the mind. One is unhappy when one does not get what one wants. And then when one *does* get what one craves for, attachment develops to that, giving rise to more and more craving, and also to worry and fear at the thought of losing it. Thus, one remains miserable whether one gets what one craves for or not.

When one looks within, one learns, at the experiential level, that every physical or vocal action that harms others starts with an impurity in the mind, which makes one agitated and miserable. Thus, one understands that one should live a moral life—not just for the benefit of others, but also for one's own peace and happiness. Just as each of our two hands helps to wash the other, wisdom purifies morality and morality purifies wisdom.

Day 68, June 16, Ashland / Portland, Oregon

Long Days, Short Nights

During the planning stage of the tour, the small town of Ashland had seemed an insignificant stop. So the caravan crew were all surprised by the enthusiasm of the old students at the one-day course and the number of locals that flocked to Goenkaji's talk at the church the previous night.

This area in the northwest is home to an active regional committee of committed old students who organize regular group sittings, one-day courses and non-center ten-day courses.

They came to the campground to meet Goenkaji and to talk with him in small groups in his motor home.

Three of the caravan crew had spent all of the previous day doing maintenance work on Goenkaji's motor home. When they retired for the night there was still about an hour of work left to do. So, as Goenkaji met the local Dhamma workers in the morning, they finished their work. When Goenkaji had finished his interviews the caravan was were ready for departure.

It was after 8 p.m. when the Dhamma caravan arrived at the RV Park south of Portland. It had been a long day for all—in terms of distance as well as time. As the caravan moved northward, the days became longer and longer. Even at 9 p.m. there was still plenty of daylight.

Day 69, June 17, Dhamma Kuñja, WA

Grove of Dhamma

For the last few days rain had been falling wherever the Dhamma caravan went. This morning too, rain fell as the caravan commenced its journey towards *Dhamma Kuñja*. The caravan reached the center at 1 p.m.

The word *kuñja* means "grove." Goenkaji gave this name to the center because of the beautiful groves of pine trees there.

A ten-day course was in progress within the main center property as Goenkaji arrived. Two one-day courses had also been organized for the following two days. Huge tents had been erected at the front of the property to accommodate all the one-day course students and visitors. In this way, the ten-day course was not disturbed by the lively activities on the rest of the center land.

The First Dip in the Ganges of Inner Reality

In his evening discourse on the fourth day, "Vipassana day," of a ten-day course, Goenkaji says:

> Today most of you have taken the first step on the path of Vipassana. Most of you, for the first time, have taken a dip in the Ganges of Dhamma within, in the Ganges of reality.

Otherwise, from the time you have taken birth, with open eyes you started seeing things outside, outside, outside. All the time the objects outside have been so predominant for you. You never cared to know what is happening inside. Even if you tried to meditate with closed eyes, you worked with these outside objects—things, which you have read, which you have heard, which you have seen. You contemplated all these. You never tried to observe the reality as it is. The reality as it is, within the framework of the body, is constantly changing. There is no stationary object on which you can keep your attention fixed. It is very helpful to know that everything is changing. Now you are becoming aware of this within the framework of the body. This is what the Buddha called, in the language of those days, *niccaṃ kāyagatā sati*.

The new students on the ten-day course in *Dhamma Kuñja* were fortunate to learn Vipassana in the presence of the master himself. Having arrived before 1 p.m., Goenkaji was able to lead the Vipassana session at 3 p.m.

After the Vipassana instructions, Goenkaji met with trust members from *Dhamma Kuñja*, who had many questions relating to the ongoing construction at the center. Amongst other things, Goenkaji emphasized the importance of using donation money carefully.

Day 70, June 18, Dhamma Kuñja, WA / Portland, Oregon / Dhamma Kuñja, WA

Noble Silence

It continued to rain at *Dhamma Kuñja*. In the morning, Goenkaji gave a telephone interview to a radio station in Mendocino, California. The station requested that he use a fixed telephone line, due to the inconsistent voice quality of mobile phones, so Goenkaji left his motor home and gave the interview at the small house at the entrance to the center.

Goenkaji was asked about silence on a Vipassana course. Wasn't it difficult? A participant in a Vipassana course is expected to maintain "noble silence" for the first nine days of the course, during which no communication is allowed amongst students. (Of course, students are free to speak to the assistant teachers to get clarification of the technique.) No reading or writing is permitted either. These rules allow students to work seriously and continuously with minimal distraction. Some course participants may have difficulty in the beginning, but they gradually start to enjoy the silence.

Ashoka: A Shining Star in the Galaxy of Rulers

In the interview Goenkaji gave the example of Ashoka to show how the Buddha's teaching has the potential to help the whole world. Ashoka had a huge empire that covered virtually the whole of the Indian subcontinent, and extended from modern day Afghanistan in the west to Bangladesh in the east. He promoted the Buddha's teaching within his empire on a massive scale. During his reign of more than 25 years, a diversity of religious sects lived together in peace. There were no communal riots. There were no invasions of foreign lands. In fact, in one of his famous rock edicts he assured his neighbors that he had no imperial ambitions, saying that his only wish was that they follow Dhamma, which he often described as righteous living.

Once, Ashoka himself spent three months on retreat in what is today Rajasthan—more than 1000 miles from his capital of Pataliputra (Patna)—to practice meditation intensively. It was a testament to the efficiency of the administration he had established that his empire remained secure, safe and peaceful for the entire time that he was away.

Everyone Has a Seed of Enlightenment

To another question, Goenkaji explained that while everyone has the potential to become fully enlightened, the path of Dhamma requires serious work. In a ten-day course only a beginning can be made.

Every moment of awareness with equanimity is an enlightening moment. As we accumulate more and more such moments, we inch towards the goal of full enlightenment.

After the interview, Goenkaji answered questions from students on the one-day course, held in a huge tent that was set up to serve as a meditation hall for his visit.

Escape Is No Solution

In the evening, Goenkaji returned to Portland where a large crowd gathered at the Smith Memorial Center Hall at Portland State University to listen to his practical wisdom.

It's clear that when we do not get something that we want, we become miserable. But even when we *do* get something that we want, we never remain satisfied with that—we immediately start craving for more. We are gripped by a desire to hang on to the object of desire and to intensify it or multiply it. While we may enjoy many things in life—like sensual pleasures, status, fame and power—any delight with these things is inevitably accompanied by an anxiety about losing them. And so we cling fiercely to these pleasurable experiences.

In one form or another, we have to confront misery in life. But how should we confront it? A common response is to distract ourselves with some form of sensual pleasure. Or we might pray. Or perhaps practice a meditation technique that concentrates the mind on some external object. All these strategies work by trying to divert the attention from the reality of the mind-matter phenomenon. But as the Enlightened One discovered, escape is no solution.

Vipassana is not mere concentration. It is awareness of all that happens in the mind-matter phenomenon, especially sensations, which are the meeting point of the mind and the body. Vipassana is to face the reality of ourselves in order to eliminate the defilements that make us miserable.

To a question about death, Goenkaji explained that if one learns the art of living a happy and peaceful life then one automatically learns the art of dying peacefully too.

Day 71, June 19, Dhamma Kuñja, WA / Lacey, WA
Know Thyself

The rain finally stopped and bright sunshine shone from early morning. A second consecutive one-day course was held at *Dhamma Kuñja*. The students on this course were told at the time of registration that Goenkaji could not be present during their course. In the end, however, Goenkaji decided to preside over the Vipassana sitting of the course, and also to answer students' questions. He then offered personal interviews.

In the evening, Goenkaji traveled to St. Martin's College in Lacey to give a public talk in the campus basketball stadium. When Goenkaji speaks at a public talk the audience usually falls into absolute silence, maintaining an almost "pin drop" silence. People listen to him with intense absorption. This stadium may never before have witnessed a large gathering that remained so quiet for so long!

At some venues early in the tour, there were problems with the audio system. But as the tour progressed, local organizers and caravan crew members took great efforts to ensure that the public address system at every public talk venue worked well. This effort resulted in a noticeable improvement in the sound quality during Goenakji's talks.

At St. Martin's, Goenkaji explained that the purpose of Vipassana is to generate, uphold and enhance human values—that the purpose of spirituality is to live a happy and harmonious life. Before the Buddha, the process by which we generate the mental impurities that prevent us from enjoying real peace and happiness was not fully understood. Only two dimensions of this process were known—our internal sense doors and the world of external sense objects. The Buddha's crucial discovery was that a third dimension—the physical sensations on the body—is needed to give us a complete understanding of how we behave.

Narrating how he came into contact with the Buddha's teaching, Goenkaji told the audience that his migraine was a blessing in disguise, because it brought him into contact with Sayagyi U Ba Khin for the first time.

When he took his first ten-day course he realized what sages all over the world mean when they say, "know thyself." Before Vipassana, he would often think, "What is this 'know thyself'? Of course, I know myself. I am Goenka. S. N. Goenka!" After Vipassana he understood the true meaning of "know thyself". In Vipassana, one understands oneself not just at the intellectual level but also at the experiential level. One finally comes to understand the truth about this mind-matter phenomenon that one has come to regard as "I" or "mine."

Meditation Postures

Many people believe that it is necessary to sit cross-legged for meditation, and some may even hesitate to join a Vipassana course for this reason. The cross-legged posture is well suited to meditation because it offers stability to the body and can be maintained for relatively long periods of time. However, meditation can be effectively practiced in any posture that one can maintain comfortably for a reasonable length of time. Anyone with a disease or disability that necessitates the use of a backrest or chair can be provided with these aids during a course. It should be clear that Vipassana is not a physical exercise. The purpose of practicing Vipassana is to train one's mind—not to torture the body. Hence, there is no insistence on any particular posture. Whatever the selected posture, however, it is important to keeps one's neck and back straight.

Due to the nature of the purification process, discomfort may be experienced even in a seemingly comfortable posture. This is because, when an old *saṅkhāra* (mental complex or conditioning) of aversion comes up to the surface of the mind, it manifests as unpleasant sensations on the body.

Painful sensations are not always due to mental impurities rising up in the mind—they can also be due to one or more other factors, such as posture, weather, diet or disease. Regardless, it is important to remember that whatever the cause of sensations, one should observe them with equanimity to avoid creating any new *saṅkhāras* (conditioning).

Instant Justice

Vipassana makes one realize the law of nature within oneself. The law is that a pure mind is full of love and compassion. A pure mind is naturally happy and peaceful, while a defiled mind remains agitated and miserable. When one breaks the law of the country, one is punished. Sometimes one may escape punishment even after breaking the law of the country. But the law of nature is always operative and inescapable. When one generates any defilement in the mind, such as anger, hatred, ill-will or jealousy, one becomes unhappy and miserable then and there.

One of the questions at the end of the talk was about combining Hatha Yoga and Vipassana. Goenkaji replied that a Vipassana practitioner can happily practice Hatha Yoga as long as one practices only the *āsanas* (postures) and *prāṇāyāma*. It is important, however, that meditation practices or mental techniques from Yoga should not be mixed with Vipassana.

One meditator wanted to know how to differentiate between a pain that is due to a physical disease or injury, and a painful sensation due to past *saṅkhāras* (conditionings). Goenkaji explained that observing sensations with equanimity does not mean that one should forsake common sense and neglect to seek medical treatment if needed. However, whether the pain is due to a disease or not, it is important to maintain equanimity towards it. Even if a pain is due to a physical ailment, reacting with aversion will generate new *saṅkhāras*, thus producing further misery for oneself. The ideal approach is to maintain equanimity towards the pain while seeking proper medical treatment for any disorder there may be. The sensations that we feel can be due to past *saṅkhāras* (during meditation, this is the case most of the time but not always), atmospheric conditions, food, posture or physical disorders. In every case, a good meditator is careful not to generate new *saṅkhāras*.

After the talk Goenkaji ate his dinner in the motor home in the parking lot. The caravan then drove for two hours to reach the house of a meditator couple, where it would settle for a stay of three days.

Day 72, June 20, Seattle
Recipe for Success, Recipe for Misery
In the morning, Goenkaji was due to give a talk to business people at Seattle's prestigious Rainier Club. He had been invited to speak there by Gair Crutcher, a local Vipassana teacher. Her family was hosting the event in memory of her late father, who had been a member of the club.

The sky was clear and Mt. Rainier could be seen clearly in all its beauty and majesty as Goenkaji was driven from his motor home to the club in downtown Seattle.

The room was full, with invited members of the Seattle business community. In his brief address, Goenkaji talked about his own life before and after Vipassana.

> Worldly success at an early age made me so tense and miserable. I would often smile in social situations, maintaining a façade of politeness even when I was extremely angry inside. Then this anger would explode once I reached home. My family members bore the brunt of it and suffered as a result.
>
> Before Vipassana, I was a bad example of a CEO. I used to believe that I was successful because my employees were afraid of me. I was a total terror to my staff and felt that if I made my employees fearful I could get more work out of them. I didn't know that life could be better. I didn't know that I could work more and in a more efficient manner. At times when I realized how miserable I was, I would cry in my prayer room in front of the idols of gods. But going out into the world, I would again be angry and miserable.

Recipe for Happiness, Recipe for Success
> Vipassana taught me self-awareness. This inner awareness brought me in touch with the truth outside, which led me to

greater worldly success. More importantly, as I became aware of the truth inside I began to enjoy immense peace and happiness.

After I started practicing Vipassana, my whole attitude changed. I started to regard my staff as collaborators in my business. I began to really care for their welfare. My business expanded. My turnover increased. I became more successful. But above all, I became more peaceful. The Buddha's teaching brought light into my life.

Proper Charity

Even a meritorious deed such as giving a donation becomes corrupt if one's volition is not right. One may give big donations merely to show the world that one is a big philanthropist. One is concerned mainly about getting name and recognition through one's donations. When one has learned how to give charity properly, the only volition is to help others, without expecting anything in return.

Meditation and Cults

In the question-and-answer session, Goenkaji was asked how to judge a particular teaching and teacher, because meditation is often associated with cults and gurus that exploit their followers. Goenkaji assured the audience that Vipassana was not a cult and that there was no scope for blind obedience in Vipassana.

- Vipassana is not a cult and it has none of the characteristics of a cult.
- There is no coercion to join or pressure to remain a meditator.
- One is asked to judge the technique for oneself, after giving it a fair trial in a ten-day course.
- No money is charged for courses and there is no question of financial exploitation by a guru.
- No teachers or organizers receive any remuneration for their service.
- All donations are entirely voluntary, without the slightest coercion.
- There is no blind adherence to any philosophical belief.

- Participants in a Vipassana course are encouraged to return to society and to fulfill their responsibilities.
- There is no effort to create a closed community that is shut off and separate from society in general.

Day 73, June 21, Seattle, WA
Knock Out Punch

Lucia Meijer was the director of the North Rehabilitation Facility (NRF), a minimum-security correctional facility in Seattle, when she began implementing Vipassana courses there about five years ago. Since that time she has taken many ten-day courses herself and now gives a considerable amount of Dhamma service at *Dhamma Kuñja*. She drove Goenkaji and Mataji to NRF to join the *"mettā* day" of a ten-day course in progress there.

Goenkaji took questions from the participants as well as from the facility staff. One inmate asked, "This is a hypothetical question, but still... Suppose I am boxing. I don't have any aversion towards my opponent. And I have an opportunity to deliver a knockout punch and I can deliver it with love and compassion. What should I do?" Laughing, Goenkaji answered, "Give a knock-out punch to your mental defilements and live a happy life!"

Dhamma in Town Halls

Buddha, the Enlightened One, traveled throughout Northern India teaching Dhamma for 45 years. Out of compassion, he often spoke of his teaching in public places in the towns he passed through. Since then, many Dhamma teachers have followed his good example by traveling far and wide to teach Dhamma in all kinds of places.

During the current Meditation Now tour, Goenkaji is speaking at a wide variety of public venues in towns across North America. That evening, Goenkaji was scheduled to give a public talk at the Seattle Town Hall.

Outer Shell and Inner Essence

All religions teach living a moral and upright life. Morality and purity of mind are the common essence of all religions. Sayagyi U Ba Khin used to say, "Purity of mind is the greatest common denominator of all religions." It is the inner essence of all religions. Rites, rituals, ceremonies, festivals, dogmas and philosophical beliefs are the outer shell of all religions. Unfortunately, most of the so-called followers of religions ignore the inner essence and give importance to the outer shell. This attachment to the outer shell causes conflict. In Vipassana one finds the common essence of all religions. It is a scientific way of observation—that is, objective observation without allowing our beliefs or past experiences to color that observation.

A ten-day course in Vipassana is the beginning of a scientific process of self-awareness. As one starts the work of investigation inside, one soon realizes that one remains unhappy because one generates defilements in the mind. All defilements such as anger, hatred, jealousy, ego, fear and lust are the products of craving and aversion.

One needs to work patiently and persistently. And then one keeps checking whether the practice is helping in daily life.

Day 74, June 22, Seattle, WA
Dhamma Prison

In his public talk in Ashland, Oregon, Goenkaji had explained that a spiritual prison of ten days is necessary to learn Vipassana, because to learn the technique properly it is necessary to practice continuously.

Vipassana has greatly helped many of the past and current inmates of the North Rehabilitation Center in Seattle. "It was almost as if I was here by divine appointment," said one ex-inmate while speaking during Goenkaji's second visit to NRF, to attend a "graduation ceremony" for inmates on the final day of a ten-day course. Many former inmates had also come, to give accounts of their experiences. One ex-inmate concisely summed up the practical nature of Vipassana, saying, "It works if you work! Try it."

Goenkaji gave a brief talk at the gathering.

Often in life one feels that one is alone and helpless. But once one learns Vipassana one acquires two great friends—Anapana and Vipassana—that are ready to help one at any time. These friends help one to keep in touch with oneself.

Time and again, research has shown that merely taking criminals off the streets and placing them behind bars reduces neither crime nor recidivism. Playing on the fact that prisons in the U.S. are often called "correctional" facilities, Goenkaji told the inmates, "No one else can correct you—you have to correct yourself."

Meeting Goenkaji was a joyous occasion for the NRF inmates. When one inmate asked where true power comes from, Goenkaji replied that it comes from within. By purging all negativities from the mind, one attains immeasurable power.

Echoing Goenkaji's statements about how to exert a positive influence on others, one inmate declared, "When you shine, people around you shine."

Neither Mahayana nor Hinayana: Dhammayana

Goenkaji was invited to speak at the Evergreen Buddhist Temple in Kirkland, Washington. His talk was simultaneously translated into Mandarin by an old student.

Goenkaji talked about Sakyamuni Buddha's crucial discovery of Vipassana—the technique by which he was able to reach perfect purity and liberation—which he distributed freely to so many over the following 45 years.

To a question on whether Vipassana is closer to Mahayana or Hinayana, Goenkaji explained that it is neither Mahayana nor Hinayana—it is Dhammayana. Sakyamuni Buddha taught neither Mahayana nor Hinayana. He taught "Dhammayana". Later on, different branches developed but the fundamental teaching of the Buddha, such as the Four Noble Truths, the *Tilakkhana* (the three fundamental characteristics of existence:

impermanence, suffering and non-self), the Noble Eightfold Path and *Paticcasamuppāda* (Dependent Origination) are accepted by all the different schools of Buddhism. These schools are like different branches of the one tree, in that they all take their nutrition from the same basic teachings of the Buddha, of which Vipassana is the quintessence.

The Buddha's followers all accept the law of cause and effect—that was his great discovery. In Vipassana, one experiences how cause and effect work—how a cause is bound to result in an effect, and then how this effect becomes the cause for yet another effect. This is how the chain of misery continues. Fortunately, the Buddha discovered the "missing link"—bodily sensations—where this cycle of cause and effect can be broken.

Vipassana is a process of training oneself to break the cycle of misery at this crucial link of sensations, by systematically learning to observe the sensations and remain impartial to them by understanding their impermanent nature.

The practice of Vipassana was preserved through the centuries by a long chain of teachers in Myanmar (Burma). Goenkaji learned Vipassana from Sayagyi U Ba Khin, who was the current heir of this great legacy. Sayagyi felt immense gratitude to India, because it was from India that Myanmar had received the jewel of Vipassana. Sayagyi used to say that India had become bankrupt, in that it had lost its greatest spiritual treasure—Vipassana. He very much wanted to take Vipassana back to India, and from there see it spread to the rest of the world. Due to circumstances, however, he was not able to carry this out himself. But when his disciple, Goenkaji, was able to go to India, he felt immense joy to know that Myanmar's debt of Dhamma would be paid back to India.

Later a question about the Bodhisatva vow arose. Goenkaji explained that a Bodhisatva (*Bodhisatta*) vow is taken in the presence of a living *Sammā Sambuddha* (Fully Enlightened One). The *Sammā Sambuddha* checks to make sure that the person who is taking the vow is sincere and has all the requisite qualities and determination to strive for Buddhahood. Only then does he pronounce this person a Bodhisatva. Whether someone has taken the Bodhisatva vow, or whether one is practicing to become an *arahat*, the essential thing is to make every effort to purify the mind, in order to accumulate the *paramīs* needed to become an *arahat* or a Bodhisatva. Rather than wasting one's time in speculations, one should work to purify the mind.

Day 75, June 23, Seattle, WA, U.S.A. / Vancouver, BC, Canada

A Gurudwara in Canada

Goenkaji set off from Seattle to Vancouver. Due to a delay at the border crossing, it was 4 p.m. when he reached Vancouver.

That evening, he gave a public talk in Hindi to a crowded hall at the Guru Ravidass Community Center Gurudwara. Goenkaji has great reverence for Guru Nanak Dev and often quotes him in the Hindi discourses played during ten-day Vipassana retreats.

From the age of 8 to 16, Goenkaji studied at a Khalsa school, where most of his schoolteachers were Sikhs. Sometimes he would go to the *sangat* in the local *gurudwara* (Sikh temple) and listen to *Guruwani* (verses from Granth Sahib, the holy book of Sikhs). After he learned Vipassana, he recollected many of the verses he had learned as a child. With the practice of Vipassana, the meanings of these verses became much clearer to him.

He explained how the Sikh Gurus had broken down the abominable caste system. He then quoted the Buddha, "Just as the waters of different rivers after merging into the great sea have no separate identity, there is no division of class and caste among those who follow Dhamma."

Guru Nanak Dev is a shining star in the sky of Indian spirituality. Goenkaji pointed out that not only did he show by his own example that a householder can be a great spiritual person, but he also established a tradition of householder spiritual teachers.

He recounted how one of his schoolteachers had explained the meaning behind the five items (*kakkas*) that Sikhs are traditionally required to carry on their person—long hair and beard, so that all look similar and can be quickly identified as brave warriors; a comb, to keep the hair clean and avoid looking like a matted hair ascetic; a sword to fight against injustice; an undergarment, as a reminder that power comes with the responsibility not to take advantage of women; and a steel bracelet, as a reminder to not harm innocent men, women and children. As soon as he raises his sword, the bracelet comes into view to remind him of his responsibility.

Dharma is Not for Power, it is for Purity

Guru Nanak Dev was very careful to prevent his followers becoming corrupted by power, money, fame or success. Vipassana can help in this, because it brings purity of mind and protection against all these intoxicating forces. Commenting on the hankering for power that is seen in so many so-called spiritual traditions, Goenkaji stated that Dharma is not for power, it is for purity.

Such was the enthusiasm of the audience that despite his long day of travel, Goenkaji's talk and question-and-answer session lasted more than two hours.

Day 76, June 24, Vancouver, BC
No Guru This

In the morning, Goenkaji went to be interviewed at the studios of IT Productions in Vancouver. The interviewer asked him how he felt about all the adulation and admiration that comes his way because he is a renowned guru. Goenkaji said that the adulation and admiration were inconsequential. "I don't consider myself a guru in the sense of a guru who will liberate you if you surrender to him. Such gurus see their followers as weak people who must depend on others for their liberation. As such they often exploit their followers.

"My role and that of any Dharma teacher is that of a guide—one who has experienced the path of Dharma, and benefited from it—someone who shows the path to others."

Goenkaji has repeatedly pointed out that a Dhamma teacher is a giver-of-the-path (*mārgadātā*), not a giver-of-liberation (*muktidātā*). This is what the Buddha declared about himself—

tumhehi kiccaṃ ātappaṃ, akkhātāro tathāgatā. One who has walked on the path and become liberated can point out the path, but one must walk on the path oneself; one must do the work of liberation oneself.

Before he passed away the Buddha exhorted his followers with the words, *attadīpā viharatha attasaraṇā anaññasaraṇā, dhammadīpā dhammasaraṇā anaññasaraṇā.* "Make yourself an island, seek refuge in yourself, not in anything else; make an island of Dhamma; seek refuge in Dhamma and not in anything else."

Goenkaji was also questioned on his relationship with Sayagyi, for example about his devotion to his teacher. Although Goenkaji was impressed by Sayagyi's saintly nature right from the first meeting, a teacher-disciple relationship was only established after he took a ten-day course under Sayagyi's guidance. As he walked further on the path of Dhamma, his respect for Sayagyi expanded steadily, and he developed an immense sense of gratitude towards him.

It is only natural to feel respect and gratitude to a teacher, but a real teacher derives happiness not by seeing his disciples worship him, but rather by seeing them follow his teaching.

The Clock of Vipassana Has Struck

Many years ago, when there were no more than a few hundred Vipassana meditators around the world in this tradition, and the courses he was teaching were small, Sayagyi U Ba Khin confidently declared that the "clock of Vipassana" had struck. This evening, as Goenkaji arrived to give a talk at the Plaza of Nations in Vancouver, it was again clear that Sayagyi was correct.

Although this was his first visit to Vancouver, a huge crowd had gathered to hear Goenkaji at this waterfront venue, proving that the wave of interest in Vipassana is spreading. The audience listened intently as Goenkaji eloquently outlined the wonders of Dhamma.

He explained that although Vipassana is widely known as a technique of meditation, it is actually a means of objective observation—or observation in a special way. While most meditation techniques aim merely to concentrate the mind, Vipassana is concerned with observing the changing nature of the body and mind. Other meditation (concentration) techniques do not involve any awareness of the reality of the mind-matter phenomenon, which out of ignorance we regard as "I" or "mine." Vipassana is awareness of the interaction between mind and matter at the experiential level, that is, at the level of physical sensations. It is self-awareness within the framework of the body.

A Deep Surgical Operation

Goenkaji often refers to a ten-day Vipassana course as a deep surgical operation of the mind. In a course, one can reach down to the depth of the mind where mental impurities arise and multiply, and where they can be eradicated.

Courses start with observation of the breath—normal, natural breath, as it is. Then, when the mind becomes sharp enough to feel the sensations, one moves on to Vipassana. This practice involves feeling sensations throughout the body and learning not to react to them with craving or aversion.

While it is easy to understand all this intellectually, mental purification comes only from the experiential wisdom that develops out of serious, intensive practice.

Day 77, June 25, Vancouver, BC

Broadcasting Dhamma

Goenkaji had given numerous radio interviews since his arrival in North America. In Vancouver, he was a featured guest on Rafe Mair's program on CKNW. Goenkaji explained how 26 centuries ago the Buddha discovered the technique of Vipassana, by exploring the reality within the framework of the body. Rafe asked whether Goenkaji's family had noticed any changes in him after he started Vipassana. "Well, of course, the results are here and now," replied Goenkaji.

As a radio talk show host dealing with controversial issues and people, the host wondered how he could do his job without getting angry—how he could express his concerns without getting heated or agitated? With a laugh, Goenkaji pointed out that when the habit of blind reaction is eliminated, all that remains is positive action. And this enables people to articulate their concerns more effectively. With Vipassana it is possible to take strong physical or vocal action, as and when it is necessary, without erupting in anger. Vipassana does not make people inactive—on the contrary, it makes them more active. All that is lost is the habit of blind reaction.

The Eightfold Noble Path

In the evening, Goenkaji returned to the Plaza of Nations to give a Dhamma discourse to the community of Chinese expatriates, which is displaying a growing interest in Vipassana—the quintessence of Sakyamuni Buddha's teaching.

Goenkaji described how Vipassana is the essence of the Noble Eightfold Path. On ten-day courses students start by taking refuge in the triple gem, and undertaking to steadfastly maintain the five precepts. This is the practice of *sīla*, which is made up of three factors:

1) *Sammā-vācā*—**Right Speech**, purity of vocal actions.

2) *Sammā-kammanta*—**Right Action**, purity of physical actions.

3) *Sammā-ājīva*—**Right Livelihood**. For the duration of a course, students live the noble life of a monk or a nun, accepting whatever is provided to them by the generosity of others. They also learn how to purify their means of livelihood when they return home, by abstaining from actions that harm others.

Students also train their minds to remain focused at a single point, without craving or aversion, in order to cultivate *samādhi*, which comprises:

4) *Sammā-vāyāma*—**Right Effort**.

5) *Sammā-sati*—**Right Awareness**. This means awareness of the reality of the present moment, because only the present can be experienced directly—past and future can only be known as memories, or as aspirations, apprehensions, or imaginings. To cultivate *sammā-sati*, students train themselves to maintain awareness of the reality that manifests at the present moment within the limited area between the nostrils and upper lip. In this way they develop awareness of the entire reality of mind and matter, from the gross to the subtle. And within a few days, they start to feel sensations throughout the body.

6) *Sammā-samādhi*—**Right Concentration**. This means continuity of awareness, from moment to moment, of the present reality. That is, the object of meditation must be pure. Goenkaji knew clearly from his own experience that meditating with mantras or visualization makes it very easy to concentrate the mind. But when he encountered Sayagyi U Ba Khin, he was asked to observe natural breath. That is because the aim of Vipassana is not merely to concentrate the mind, but also to purify it. *Sammā-samādhi* is essential for cultivating *paññā* (experiential wisdom or insight) and enjoying the authentic happiness of mental purity.

The practice of *paññā* consists of two path factors:

7) *Sammā-saṅkappa*—**Right Thoughts**. It is not that all thought must stop in order to cultivate *paññā* (wisdom), but with practice, the pattern of thought changes entirely. Instead of thoughts of craving, aversion, and delusion, the mind dwells more and more in wholesome thoughts of love, compassion, Dhamma and the path of true purification.

8) *Sammā-diṭṭhi*—**Right Understanding**. This means real *paññā*, wisdom—the understanding of reality as it is, not just as it appears to be.

The *tilakkhaṇa* (the three characteristics of all existence) of impermanence, suffering and non-self, are not mere philosophical beliefs—they characterize the nature of all conditioned things. These three characteristics can be readily experienced by each and every person who takes a few steps on the scientific path of exploration laid down by the Buddha. Thus, these three characteristics should never be understood as any kind of Buddhist dogma or philosophy. The Buddha declared repeatedly that his teaching was above and beyond all philosophies.

Siddhartha Gotama discovered and proclaimed the truth of existence—which is indisputably applicable to one and all. This truth, this *dhamma*, is not something that applies only to Buddhists. Mere faith or belief in *anattā* (no-self) does not eliminate the habit of reacting with craving and aversion to pleasant and unpleasant experiences. Only a penetrating investigation within can reveal that everything in the field of mind and matter is ephemeral and without any essence. If there is an "I" anywhere inside, then one should have control over the flow of mind and matter. A meditator finds, however, that there is no control to be had over these phenomena. Out of ignorance, one remains in the grip of the delusion that there is a self, when the truth is that a person consists of five aggregates, all of which are in a constant flux, and therefore without any essence. *Anattā* is not a philosophy—it is something to be experienced.

Suññatā (Shunyatā)

Suññatā has two meanings. First, it means that everything in the field of mind and matter is devoid of any lasting essence or substance that one might cling to and understand to be "I" or "mine" or "my soul." Secondly, the experience of *nibbāna* is referred to as *suñña*.

Goenkaji concluded his talk by humbly encouraging the followers of the different branches of Buddhism, and also people of other religious backgrounds, to learn the practical aspect of the Buddha's teaching.

Day 78, June 26, Vancouver, BC, / Victoria
Dāna of Food

Throughout the long tour of North America, numerous expatriate Indian meditators lovingly cooked Indian vegetarian meals for Goenkaji and Mataji, thus enabling their teachers to eat as their health required while they traversed the continent to disseminate Dhamma. Today, Goenkaji and Mataji met with and thanked the meditators who cooked for them during their stay in Vancouver. They called these Indian women *annapurnas* (literally, those who give food). (In some parts of India, Annapurna is a common female name.)

These selfless volunteers cooked not only for Goenakji and Mataji but also for the caravan members who traveled with them. Despite having traveled closely with Goenkaji for weeks and weeks, many of the crew members did not seek a single private meeting with Goenkaji, so as not to take up his precious time.

In countries that have traditionally followed the Buddha's teaching, lay people regularly offer food to those who have renounced the householder's life to pursue the practice of Dhamma as fully as possible. From his time in Myanmar, Goenkaji often talks of how wonderful he felt to see *bhikkhus*, very early in the morning, going on alms round in a single file with measured steps and downcast eyes. The householders understand that the *bhikkhus* have dedicated their lives to the highest endeavor that a human being can undertake—working for liberation from all suffering. That is why they feel such great joy in serving food to them. The merit they earn from this *dāna* is in proportion to their volition—that is, to the happiness they feel in serving this food. On top of the immediate joy they bring, such wholesome acts of generosity will bring forth wonderful fruits in the future too. The same is true of any wholesome, selfless action. The merit earned is certainly not a matter of blind faith—it is a natural extension of the joy and peace felt in performing it.

The work of providing healthy food for Goenkaji and everyone else in the Dhamma caravan made a valuable contribution to Goenkaji's mission of spreading the message of Dhamma in North America.

After taking leave of the small group that had come to see Goenkaji in his motor home, the Dhamma caravan boarded the ferry from Tsawwassen to Swartz Bay on Vancouver Island. The local organizers had rented the ferry's conference room for the use of Goenkaji and the crew, so everyone gathered there after the ferry set off. From time to time, servers went outside to enjoy the beautiful views of distant snow-capped mountains. Two female servers led Mataji out to the bow to watch as the ferry threaded its way through tiny islands. Goenkaji remained inside, absorbed in his reading—the commentary to the *Mangala Sutta*.

On arrival at Vancouver Island, the Dhamma caravan drove to the Westbay Marine Village and RV Park. It was sunny but cool. In the evening, Goenkaji gave a public talk in Victoria, at the Conservatory of Music—a beautiful hall in a gorgeous stone church.

Goenkaji explained that sensations on the body are like a junction from which lead two distinct paths. By reacting with craving or aversion towards these sensations one sets out on the first of these two paths—the path of misery. By not reacting to these sensations—by simply observing them with an understanding of their impermanent nature—one sets out on the second path—the path of liberation.

Goenkaji also recounted an old story about a group of Christian missionaries who joined one of his early Vipassana courses in India. At the end of the course, an elderly nun from the group, a Mother Superior, came to him and said, "Goenkaji, you are teaching Christianity in the name of the Buddha!" Answering her with a smile, Goenkaji told her that the law of nature is the same for everyone. Suffering is universal, and so too is the way out of suffering.

Day 79, June 27, Victoria, BC

What Goenkaji Does on a Scheduled Rest Day

Rain started to fall during the night, and continued for the entire morning. Though today had been marked down as a rest day for Goenkaji, it nonetheless turned out to be a busy one:

In the morning, Goenkaji went out for a haircut. Then, despite not being scheduled to do so, he went to give Vipassana instructions at the one-day course being held at the Victoria Truth Center, He then returned to the RV Park.

In the afternoon, Goenkaji's younger sister, Mrs. Ellaïchidevi Agrawal, a Vipassana teacher, arrived from India to join the Dhamma caravan. The crew greeted her enthusiastically. Everyone was happy for Mataji because now she would have someone to speak with in Hindi. (Mataji doesn't speak English).

Goenkaji met with a few meditators during his evening walk.

After tea, Mataji and Ellaichidevi, together with some local meditators and caravan crew members went to visit the famous Butchart Gardens in Victoria. While the others were at the garden, Goenkaji gave two telephone interviews, to journalists from Missoula, Montana.

Later he granted an interview to Bennett Miller, the documentary filmmaker accompanying the Dhamma caravan.

Even past 8 p.m., it was bright outside. Since the rain continued unabated, Goenkaji decided to exercise inside the motor home.

Day 80, June 28, Victoria, BC / Chilliwack, BC
Ambitious Plan

In the morning, the Dhamma caravan made a rather late start, barely making it in time to catch the 11 a.m. ferry back to the mainland. The day's plan was to visit a nunnery for *bhikkhunis* from Hong Kong, in Chilliwack, before heading through the mountains to reach *Dhamma Surabhi* by evening.

After the ferry crossing, the caravan stopped for lunch. Rain continued to fall. Due to the continuing rain and heavy holiday-weekend traffic, the caravan traveled slowly.

It was 7 p.m. when Goenkaji arrived at the Po Lam nunnery, to be greeted by the nine *bhikkhunis* who live there. The most senior of the nuns had done a Vipassana course. All the others planned to join a ten-day course in September. Goenkaji presented the nuns with gifts of books.

Since it was still raining, the crew decided to stop for the night at the RV Park in Chilliwack.

Day 81, June 29, Chilliwack, BC / Dhamma Surabhi, Merritt
The Fragrance of Dhamma

It was still raining in Chilliwack when the Dhamma caravan left the RV Park mid-morning for the trip to *Dhamma Surabhi* (fragrance of Dhamma). The caravan crew had grown a little weary of all the rain, particularly those that had to spend the night in soggy tents. There were not even any dry places to set up the dining tables. When the word came in by telephone that it was bright and sunny at *Dhamma Surabhi*, the news was greeted with joy.

As the Dhamma caravan wove its way up into the mountains, snow could be seen here and there amongst the vivid green trees and rocky crevices. At a certain point along the beautiful mountain road, brilliant sunlight suddenly flooded down from the sky. Finally, the caravan reached *Dhamma Surabhi*.

The first phase of development at this new and very scenic Vipassana center had just been completed. As at other centers visited by the caravan, existing facilities could not accommodate all the students who had come for the scheduled one-day course, so tents were erected for use as a temporary Dhamma hall and for dining halls.

When the caravan arrived at 1 p.m., Goenkaji decided to go straight to the temporary Dhamma hall where the one-day course was in progress for a question-and-answer session. A student asked about the importance of reading Dhamma literature. Goenkaji said that reading Dhamma literature is very beneficial, because it provides inspiration, and clarification for one's practice. He warned, however, that some of the translations could cause confusion due to translation errors. It was almost 2 p.m. when Goenkaji finished answering questions.

In the evening, Goenkaji met with a freelance reporter to record an interview for a radio station, after which he met with students for private interviews. The teachers in charge of

Dhamma Surabhi then took Goenkaji and Mataji on a tour of the center's main building, which currently houses the meditation hall, kitchen and dining hall, as well as all accommodation. The group also walked around the site for some time to consider current plans for further expansion of the center. *Dhamma Surabhi* is nestled in woods along the slopes of a valley with a mountain stream of sparkling water running alongside the property.

Goenkaji then held a brief meeting with the center trust.

Day 82, June 30, Dhamma Surabhi, Merritt
Peace First: The First Nations

The native inhabitants of Canada—those who lived there before the arrival of European settlers—are often referred to as the "First Nations." In the morning, Goenkaji was visited by a group consisting of the Grand Chief of the Cold Water people, his wife and daughter, and his father (who is an Elder of the Upper Nicola as well as the Cold Water tribe). The Chief explained how his father and grandfather had taught him a meditative life and an appreciation of solitude, and how living peacefully with others is of fundamental importance to the First Nations people. Goenkaji explained to him how peace of mind puts us in perfect harmony with nature. He also explained how Vipassana can cure various kinds of addiction and how it helps to eliminate impurities such as anger, hatred and fear. He exhorted the visitors to try the technique, so that they might gain not only a better understanding of their ancient culture, but also a powerful tool to help them preserve it.

Goenkaji mentioned how many Maoris (pre-European inhabitants of New Zealand) have benefited from Vipassana. It all started after one or two prominent members of the Maori community joined a Vipassana course and began spreading word of its unique value within their community.

Immediately after the meeting with the First Nations a business reporter for the Chicago Tribune called to seek a telephone interview. Goenkaji told him how Vipassana helps people to strike a balance in life, even as they are striving for business success. The reporter wanted to know why charging money for Dharma teachings was wrong. Goenkaji explained that since Dharma is priceless, putting a price tag on it would devalue it. Moreover, when people start charging for their teaching, money soon becomes their principal motivation. Rather than a selfless service, done out of love and compassion, it becomes a commercial enterprise. Trying to make a profit is fine in business, but in Dharma it is a poison that kills the very essence of Dharma.

Before winding up a long morning session, Goenkaji gave some more private interviews.

In the early evening, Goenkaji again met individually with meditators. From 9 to 10 p.m. Goenkaji gave the opening formalities and Anapana instructions for the ten-day course starting that day at *Dhamma Surabhi*, which was full to capacity. He then led the customary evening *mettā* session with the servers at the center, and took a few phone calls. It was after 11 p.m. when Goenkaji retired to his motor home.

Day 83, July 1, Dhamma Surabhi, Merritt / Golden

Into Nature

Goenkaji's inaugural visit to British Columbia generated far more public interest than expected. It also served to bring together a great number of local meditators.

It was fascinating and inspiring to observe the many and various people that gathered to hear the profound, yet simple wisdom of Vipassana. It is quite easy to incite crowds with inflammatory speeches, expressions of religious fervor and the like, but getting people to quietly look within themselves is very difficult indeed. Though simple and logical, Dhamma is also serious and profound. It is clear that the clock of Vipassana has definitely struck in this part of the world.

The meditators serving on the Dhamma caravan were extremely pleased with the response to Goenkaji's visit. *Dhamma Surabhi* was living up to its name. The *surabhi* (fragrance) of Dhamma was wafting throughout the state of British Columbia.

The caravan left the pretty Cold Water Valley in the morning. On both sides of the road the mountains were dressed with the lush green of pines, giant cedars and firs. As the small convoy climbed through the Canadian Rockies it came upon one breathtaking vista after another. The air was pleasantly cool. The verdant forests on each side evoked a meditative mood. Every now and then treeless, rocky mountaintops raised their heads, each with some snow atop them. In the Glacier National Park the snow flowed in rivulets down the mountain gorges.

This day was devoted entirely to travel. There were no scheduled events pressing the caravan to reach its destination. After a hectic program from San Diego to *Dhamma Surabhi*, the crew was able to sit back and relax a little. After passing through the Glacier National Park, Goenkaji emerged from his motor home to walk in the quiet, cool mountain air.

It was after 9 p.m. when the caravan reached the sleepy little town of Golden. By the time the caravan crew finished setting up for the night it was quite late. Before sleeping they meditated in small groups in the various tents, pop-up trailers and motor homes. The latest of the groups finished its sitting at about 1 a.m.

Day 84, July 2, Golden / Calgary
The Mighty Rockies

Daylight broke early, but the caravan crew was compensated for the night's shortness by a breathtaking view of snow-peaked mountains, and the pleasant gurgling of the nearby Kicking Horse river. Although it was a long way to the next tour destination, the late night had made the preparations somewhat sluggish. Some crew members decided to take advantage of the clean cool mountain air to jog, walk or bike. One server headed towards the town's lone Internet café, close to the park, to retrieve news for Goenkaji. The caravan had now been in remote parts for quite a long time, so Goenkaji needed to catch up with important news from Vipassana organizations around the world, as well as with ordinary world news.

The caravan finally rolled out of the park at around 11 a.m. Some of the most beautiful scenery of the tour was on this stretch. All along the way there were turquoise mountain lakes, trees of vivid green, crystal clear creeks and inviting rivers. The caravan stopped for lunch at the famous Lake Louise, a serene glacial lake. The Rocky Mountains had been encountered in all their grandeur. At times they were draped with the soothing foliage of woodlands—at times they were bare, steel gray masses. With or without snow they were always grand.

One huge, gray mountain that the caravan skirted near Banff exuded an air of remarkable solidity and stability. A crew member recollected the Dhammapada verse:

Selo yathā ekaghano, vātena na samīrati;
evaṃ nindāpasaṃsāsu, na samiñjanti paṇḍitā.
Like a solid rock that remains unshaken by the wind;
A wise person is not affected by praise and criticism.

The mountains appeared to extend without end on either side of the road, but suddenly, in the late afternoon, the caravan hit the plains outlying the city of Calgary, reaching the RV Park around 6 p.m. Despite the late hour, the sun was still beating down like on a mid-summer afternoon in India.

The crew busied themselves with various chores. Goenkaji was spotted walking up a steep slope on his own just after 9 p.m.

Day 85, July 3, Calgary
Stampede

As it happened, Calgary was hosting its annual fair and rodeo show, known as the Calgary Stampede.

While most beings in the world stampede from birth to death, in one life after another, some—those with "little dust in their eyes"—develop the urge to break free of this cycle of misery. A meditator comes to realize that there is no greater stampede than the stampede of thoughts in the mind.

An enthusiastic group of local meditators, including trust members and assistant teachers, came to the RV Park in the morning to meet with Goenkaji and ask him questions.

Committed Relationships: Doors are Closed

One of the requirements for admission to a long Vipassana course (of 20 days or more) is that a person be either single and celibate or in a committed relationship. One of the students asked the meaning of the term "committed relationship". Goenkaji explained that it means a relationship based on a lifelong commitment—a relationship where the doors are closed.

In the evening, Goenkaji spoke at the Metropolitan Center in downtown Calgary. In anticipation of a large crowd, the organizers had arranged a simulcast of Goenkaji's talk in an adjacent room for those who could not be seated in the main hall. When it became clear that the main hall would overflow, old students were asked to go and watch the talk next door, to allow newcomers the opportunity to listen to Goenkaji live. Eventually, even the smaller room filled up, so that some people had to stand.

Meditation versus Vipassana

Although this technique is commonly described as Vipassana meditation, the word meditation can be misleading, because it commonly means the practice of concentrating the mind on a stationary object. In Vipassana, one observes the constantly changing reality within, as it manifests itself from moment to moment. In this sense, Vipassana is quite different to other forms of meditation.

With Eyes Closed

Goenkaji went on to describe what is practiced in a ten-day Vipassana course. He told the audience that one starts by sitting down in a comfortable posture, with eyes gently closed. The eyes serve no function in the awareness of breath and sensations. If they are left open, the mind is certain to be distracted. Thus, the eyes should remain closed during meditation.

The Breath: A Bridge to the Unknown

If, along with awareness of breath, one repeats a word, a mantra or the name of a god; or if one visualizes a deity or other form, the mind gets concentrated faster and more easily. In Vipassana, though, one observes bare respiration, as it naturally is—without any control, and without the addition of any word or visual form.

Such aids are not permitted because the final aim of Vipassana is not merely to concentrate the mind. Concentration is just a means—a step to the greater goal of total purification of mind, and liberation from all misery.

With an imagined or external object of meditation, such as a word or visual form, it is not possible to discover the subtler truths about oneself. To penetrate to subtle truths, one must begin with obvious truths. That is why the work of meditation begins with respiration—the most gross, apparent reality of the body. Respiration also has the important advantage of being available always and everywhere—from the moment of birth to the moment of death.

Vipassana is a path from the known to the unknown. Since the breath is a bodily function that can be conscious or unconscious, intentional or automatic—it serves as a bridge between these two fields. By maintaining awareness of natural, normal breath, one starts experiencing even subtler truths about oneself. And every step is a step with reality, towards the discovery of subtler realities about oneself—about one's own body and mind.

Although the breath is a physical function, it is also intimately tied to one's mental state. This means that by observing the breath, one also starts observing the mind. As soon as any impurity arises in the mind, the breath becomes abnormal—it becomes faster and harder. Then, when the impurity passes away, the breath again becomes soft. In this way, the breath functions like bridge between body and mind—a gateway to the reality of the mind-matter phenomenon.

The next step in the practice is the awareness of sensations. Vipassana is the process of observing sensations objectively—that is, without identifying with them in any way.

Peace Within First

Calgary had recently hosted a summit of the G8 nations. In his talk here, Goenkaji explained that there cannot be peace in the world unless there is peace within individuals. After all, society is nothing more than the sum of the individuals that make it up.

Goenkaji explained that the value of intellectual understanding is limited. It can provide clarification and inspiration, but the real fruits of spirituality can only be achieved by real, actual practice. He urged the audience to spare ten days of their lives to learn the wonderful technique of Vipassana. "Practice it, see the results for yourself and only then accept it!" he exhorted.

After the talk Goenkaji recorded an interview for Shaw TV, and then met with about 90 students from the SHAD program, which brings together some of the very brightest high school students in Canada.

Day 86, July 4, Calgary / Edmonton, Alberta
The Northern Point of the North American Tour

It was a hectic day. The caravan prepared early for its journey to Edmonton, the capital of Alberta (The Wild Rose Province).

In the initial planning stages of the tour, there was some hesitation about including Edmonton on the tour, as it meant that the caravan would have to travel northward from Calgary and then again southward back to Calgary. But any reservations about whether Edmonton merited a visit evaporated on seeing the enthusiastic turnout to Goenkaji's public talk at the beautiful Edmonton City Hall.

> Each and every time an impurity is generated in the mind, one becomes unhappy. One can divert one's attention from the impurity by reciting a name or visualizing a form, but this is avoiding reality. All those who explored the entire field of

mind and matter to the point of complete enlightenment understood that diverting the attention, though it may appear to push out the negativity, only serves to suppress it. While the negativity—maybe anger, hatred, ill will, lust or fear—seems to disappear from the surface level of the mind, it just gets pushed back inside, where it continues to simmer and multiply. Thus, the unhappiness persists. So, escape is clearly not a solution to the problem. These sages of the past realized that negativities must be observed. Whenever any negativity arises in the mind, it should be neither suppressed, nor allowed to express itself at the vocal or physical level. The solution lies in taking the middle path, of observing the impurity objectively. By this process, the impurity becomes weaker and weaker, until it eventually passes away.

Yet, while this is all well and good in theory, it is very difficult in practice, because negativity tends to overpower the mind very quickly when it arises. And given that it is abstract and intangible, how is it possible to observe negativity? Even if someone sits down with closed eyes, determined to observe mental impurities as they arise, what would happen? Suppose anger arises. Before one could remember to observe anything, the mind would be overcome by emotion. So what can be done?

Conceivably, one could hire a private secretary to give a reminder whenever anger arises. A single private secretary could only be on duty for one eight-hour shift, and one can never be sure when exactly anger might come! So three private secretaries would actually be needed—or maybe four or five. Even assuming that a private secretary could be on hand 24 hours a day, what would happen when anger arose. The private secretary would call out: "Watch out! Anger! Observe the anger!" Naturally, the first thing one would do is shout at him or slap him: "Shut up! Who asked you? I know what I'm doing!" Such is the nature of anger!

Even assuming one did not explode at the secretary, instead saying to him, "Thank you. You have done your job well.

Now I must observe my anger," a big problem remains. Anger has no form or color, so how does one observe it. Closing one's eyes to try and observe it would only bring to mind the object of the anger—the person or incident that aroused the anger. And thus, the drama of the anger would be replayed over and over in the mind, feeding and stimulating the anger, making the problem worse and worse. This is not observing anger.

It is precisely in order to solve this problem that the enlightened people of the past have taught us to observe our respiration and sensations. They realized that mind and matter are profoundly interconnected—that they are two sides of the same coin. As soon as anger, lust, fear, or any other negativity arises in the mind, two things start happening at the physical level—the first at a gross level, the second at a subtler level.

At the gross level, the breath loses its normality. It becomes fast or hard, or irregular. Only when the impurity subsides, does it return to normal. And something else starts in the body at a subtler level, at the level of sensations—perhaps palpitations, heat, perspiration or tension.

While it is very difficult to observe abstract impurities such as anger or lust, it is quite easy to observe breath or bodily sensations. With practice, any ordinary person can develop this ability. With a little training, this objective observation of mental impurities becomes easy. One can learn to face negativity—neither running away from it, nor suppressing it.

This is a wonderful solution, but it requires practice—mere lectures about it do not help. After all, even a child knows that anger, hatred and fear get in the way of happiness. Serious practice and work are required. There is no magic or miracle involved. The old habit pattern of the mind is to focus on the apparent, external cause of unhappiness, without trying to understand what goes on within. With Vipassana one comes to realize that what goes on within us is far more important than anything outside.

After the public talk, Goenkaji was interviewed for the TV show "Image India."

Edmonton was the northernmost point on the North America tour. Daylight persisted past 10 p.m. As Goenkaji was driven back from the public talk, three huge rainbows appeared on the horizon. One was very bright, the other two less bright. They looked like huge columns rising out of the earth, fading at their tops. No one in the caravan crew had ever seen such large rainbows. Someone suddenly spotted the other ends of the two rainbows on the left side. These also looked like columns rising from the ground. Only moments before the rainbows came into view, two crew members were talking with a local meditator about whether this part of Canada was known for the Northern Lights. Now, everyone agreed that these rainbows were almost as spectacular as seeing the Northern Lights.

Day 87, July 5, Edmonton / High River, Alberta
Success Without Dhamma Means Ego and Intolerance

Despite having a late night, Goenkaji was ready early in the morning for a talk to business people at the University of Alberta's Telus Center. The talk was co-sponsored by the Canadian Center for Social Entrepreneurship.

Goenkaji told the audience that before he learned Vipassana, worldly success had made him a very ego-centered person. As a result of his strong ego, he became very intolerant and short-tempered. He then explained how everything changed after he received the gift of Vipassana.

He remarked jokingly to a question that Dhamma is not a credit business—it is a cash business. The results come here and now. And, naturally, as one accrues merits, one's credit rating improves.

Answering another question, he pointed out that honesty is always the best policy. It is greed that makes us blind to what is in our own real interest.

While Vipassana makes people very soft within, it also enables them to take very tough action when needed.

Goenkaji recited one of his favorite little ditties:
It is easy enough to be pleasant,
When life flows like a sweet song;
But the man worthwhile,
Is the man who can smile,
When everything goes dead wrong!

Finally, Goenkaji thanked the audience for taking the time to listen to him. He reminded everyone that such talks about Dhamma could serve only to enhance one's intellectual understanding. In order to get any real benefit from Vipassana, they would have to spare ten days to go and learn the technique.

Following the talk, Goenkaji and Mataji met with local meditators at a roadside rest area just outside Edmonton. Goenkaji answered questions about various administrative matters and the possibility of starting a new center, as well as questions about the practice by individuals.

In the afternoon, the caravan left Edmonton for a campground south of Calgary.

Mosquito Misery

In the Tipiṭaka (the collection of discourses given by the Buddha and some of his chief disciples) one finds mention of *ḍaṃsa-makasa-vātā-tapa-sarīsapa-samphassānaṃ* (contact with gadflies, mosquitoes, wind and reptiles). Although a monk's robes protect him against such contacts, he is expected to tolerate these nuisances with equanimity, whenever they cannot be avoided. Of course, with the advantage of more protected environments, mosquitoes and the like are much less of a problem for the meditators of today.

Now and again, at different camping sites along the tour, the Dhamma caravan had to face the nuisance of mosquitoes. This stop had some of the fiercest mosquitoes encountered thus far on the tour. But just as the scourge of mosquitoes has persisted since the time of the Buddha, so too, thankfully, has the wonderful Dhamma.

The caravan crew set up a tent for a group sitting. Some of the servers, being too busy to join the group, did their evening sitting in the documentary filmmaker's motor home, at well past midnight.

Day 86, July 6, High River, Alberta, Canada / Whitefish, Montana
In the morning, before the caravan headed off towards its next destination, back in the U.S., Goenkaji met briefly with a local assistant teacher couple.

Rockies Again
From Edmonton and on past Calgary, the caravan traveled on a long, flat stretch of plains. For a while the Rocky Mountains could be seen in the distance to the right, but they eventually disappeared from view altogether. Those not familiar with the area might have thought the Rockies had been left behind for good. However, further on, the caravan found itself once again heading towards the mighty Rockies. For lunch the caravan stopped at a rest area, surrounded by beautiful snow-capped peaks.

The border crossing, unlike the one between Seattle and Vancouver, was small and quiet. A lone vehicle was waiting ahead of the caravan to enter the U.S. After the immigration officer graciously wished Goenkaji and Mataji a happy stay in America, the caravan headed to the property of a meditator near Whitefish, Montana.

Deer Park
The caravan left the main road for a winding dirt road. When it reached a long, pretty meadow it came to a stop. The property, featuring a house bounded by meadows at front and back, with low-forested hills behind, appeared to be an ideal place for a recluse. And in fact, a meditator had been living alone here for years. Any lack in material comfort was more than made up for up by simple, genuine hospitality, a meditative atmosphere and the richness and purity of the natural environment. Deer frolicked in the rear meadow, oblivious to the presence of so many visitors—possibly the largest human invasion the place

had ever seen. The property reminded some of the crew of the description of the *migadāva* (deer park) in Sarnath where the Buddha set in motion, the Wheel of Dhamma.

On a more mundane level, the caravan crew was happy to learn that despite its very remote location, the house had a telephone connection. This enabled them to connect their laptops to the Internet and catch up with their e-mailing.

Unfortunately the terrain was too uneven for Goenkaji to walk outside.

Day 89, July 7, Whitefish / Missoula, Montana
Open Sky

Montana is called the "Big Sky" state. The Buddha famously said: *sambādho gharāvāso rajāpatho, abbhokāso pabbajā*—the household life is a dusty path full of hindrances, while the ascetic life is like the open sky. Who would have imagined that a distinguished descendant of the Buddha would one day venture to this remote, sparsely populated corner of North America to teach householders how to clean themselves of the dust of worldly life!

All of Missoula's newspapers carried news of Goenkaji's arrival, along with articles on Vipassana. The caravan stayed on the property of a local meditator's mother, who very kindly offered the use of her house as well as her land. For the period of Goenkaji's stay she went to stay in a friend's house. All were touched by her generous gesture, especially in view of her advanced age and the inconvenience it caused her.

A leading local TV news channel had requested an interview with Goenkaji, and as soon as the caravan pulled up on the front lawn of the house, a TV crew was waiting. The reporter had time for only one question to Goenkaji before rushing off to deliver the tape to the news producer. That night many of the crew gathered in the house with local students to see Goenkaji on the 10 o'clock news.

The caravan crew were warmly greeted and sumptuously fed by the huge team of local Dhamma workers. They also delighted in watching a couple of Osprey eagles that had built a nest for three offspring on a telephone pole at the corner of the property. A herd of cows including a newborn calf lived in the field at the entrance and charmed the crew each time they passed. The infamous Montana mosquitoes too kept the caravan crew company but did not trouble them too much.

Day 98, July 8, Missoula, Montana
Rain and Sunshine
It rained in the morning but from late afternoon through to evening, it was bright and sunny.

A tent was erected on the neighboring property of a local assistant teacher for the one-day course arranged for that day. Goenkaji attended the course in the morning to give Vipassana instructions and answer questions from students.

In the evening, he gave a public talk at the University of Montana's Music Recital Hall. Once again, the large audience seemed to hang onto Goenkaji's every word.

Goenkaji spoke of the gross misery that is apparent to everyone, as well as the more fundamental suffering that underlies our attachment to the five aggregates. While talking about apparent suffering he described old age—the deterioration of the senses, having to walk with a stick, and wrinkles over the face and body. And on top of all this, for most people, the mere thought of death arouses horror.

One is miserable because of impurities in the mind. Mental impurities can be eradicated by simply observing them. This can be done by being aware of breath and bodily sensations, which are intimately connected to mental impurities—they are like two sides of the same coin. Awareness of breath or sensations allows us to face mental impurities and uproot them.

After the talk, local meditators served punch and cookies to the audience.

Day 91, July 9, Missoula / Billings, Montana
Mind Matters Most

In the morning, Goenkaji gave an interview by telephone to Minnesota Public Radio. In the discussion, he explained that at the base of all unwholesome vocal and physical actions is an unwholesome mental action. Every mental action arises simultaneously with a flow of sensations on the body.

Manopubbaṅgamā dhammā, manosetṭhā, manomayā.
Mind precedes all phenomena; mind matters most; everything is mind-made.
Manasā ce paduṭṭhena bhāsati vā karoti vā.
Tato naṃ dukkhamanveti cakkaṃ'va vahato padaṃ.
If, with an impure mind,
one performs any action of speech or body,
then suffering will follow that person,
as the cartwheel follows the foot of the draught-ox.
Manasā ce pasannena, bhāsati vā karoti vā.
Tato naṃ sukhamanveti, chāyā'va anapāyinī.
If, with a pure mind,
one performs any action of speech or body,
then happiness will follow that person,
as a shadow that never leaves.

Today was the first of three long travel days. The caravan set off just before 11 a.m., traveling uneventfully over the vast plains of Montana to a motor home park in Billings.

Day 92, July 10, Billings, Montana / Bismarck, North Dakota
Staying Together

One of the challenges of the crew on these long stretches of travel was to keep the caravan vehicles together. At times, some of the vehicles moved ahead while others lagged behind. This led to confusion, particularly if the vehicles were too far apart for the walkie-talkies to operate or if there was inadequate strength for mobile phone communication. Usually, however, the drivers of the various caravan vehicles were disciplined and well coordinated.

This day there was some minor confusion with the caravan, after communication between vehicles was lost before lunch. Eventually, the vehicles managed to come together for lunch at a rest area. The expert cook and his efficient assistant made sure that food was served as quickly as possible to Goenkaji and Mataji. Others cooked for the caravan and made sure that the crew ate without any delay.

When Goenkaji and Mataji learned that travel was behind schedule, they decided to forego the customary stop for afternoon tea. As a result, the caravan reached its destination by 8 p.m. The caravan had entered the Central Time Zone.

Day 93, July 11, Bismarck, North Dakota / Minneapolis, Minnesota

Longest Day and Another Flat Tire

This day saw the longest distance covered by the caravan on the tour whilst Goenkaji and Mataji were with it. The vehicles had traveled farther on other days when Goenkaji and Mataji were elsewhere—once when Goenkaji flew to Houston for a public talk, and the second time when he flew to New York to deliver the keynote speech at the official *Vesākha* celebrations of the United Nations.

The caravan was under some time pressure because it needed to reach the night's campsite by 9 p.m. There was some apprehension about whether it could make it in time.

The drivers applied themselves diligently to the challenge at hand. Only absolutely essential stops were made. Stops for fuel or other purposes were either minimized or eliminated. At times, the caravan split into two groups of vehicles, but the crew had learned from the communication problems of the previous day and now took care to stay in close contact. In the afternoon, the pop-up trailer attached to the kitchen motor home developed a flat tire. Fortunately, a passing driver kindly pointed it out; otherwise it might have gone unnoticed for a long time. After radio contact, the caravan crew promptly converged to quickly change the tire, and soon the caravan was on the road again.

Goenkaji was briefed on the road about outstanding correspondence. He gave instructions and clarifications in response to questions from all over the world, relating to administrative issues as well as meditation.

The caravan vehicles all reached their destination at about the same time. Local meditators arrived with food for Goenkaji and Mataji as well as the crew.

For the first time in three days, Goenkaji and Mataji were able to walk at their leisure.

Day 94, July 12, Minneapolis, MN
Twin Cities

The twin cities of St. Paul and Minneapolis are home to a strong group of Dhamma workers who have served on non-center courses in the area for years. They took the opportunity of Goenkaji's presence in their area to gather at the campground and seek his guidance on a wide variety of matters related to their practice and Dhamma service. In particular, they wanted to know whether they were ready to establish a Vipassana center. Goenkaji encouraged them to find a suitable property to serve as a center, or else to establish a Dhamma house that could be a stepping stone to a full-fledged center.

Craving: A Bottomless Bucket.

In the evening, Goenkaji gave a public talk at the University of Minnesota, in the Ted Mann Concert Hall. He described how trying to satisfy craving (*taṇhā*) is like trying to fill a bottomless bucket with water. He went on to explain the cause of craving and the process by which it can be totally uprooted.

Anicca to Anattā: A natural progress

Goenkaji stressed that the direct experience of *anicca* (impermanence) is the way to eliminate misery. As one develops awareness of sensations, their characteristic of impermanence becomes more and more obvious. This experiential wisdom of *anicca* (impermanence) then leads logically to the next step—the understanding of suffering. That which is impermanent cannot be the cause of lasting happiness. And finally, that which is impermanent and suffering cannot be regarded as "I" or "me" or "mine"—that is, as any kind of a self.

Goenkaji explained that *anattā* (non-self) is not a philosophical statement on the existence or non-existence of "soul," but rather a fundamental experiential truth of the mind-matter phenomenon, to which by deep-rooted conditioning individuals look upon as "I", "me" or "mine." With the practice of Vipassana one realizes that this entire phenomenon is ephemeral and without any core or essence—it is in a constant flux, and one has no control over it.

The experiential wisdom of *anattā* (non-self) is the logical conclusion of the understanding of *anicca* (impermanence). The more one gets established in the experience of *anicca* (impermanence), the deeper one penetrates to the wisdom of *anattā* (non-self).

Day 95, July 13, Minneapolis, MN / Chicago, IL
Why Vipassana Centers?

Today Goenkaji left early to go to the one-day course. On his return, the Dhamma caravan took off for an RV Park near Chicago. The park was packed with people enjoying their summer holidays. While most campgrounds are quiet at night, this one was noisy and boisterous. The management of the park had over-booked for the night, and the places reserved for the caravan had been given to other guests. With no other option, the caravan settled on a patch of grass at the far end of the park. Most of the caravan vehicles were not able to hook up to water or electricity. Fortunately, there was enough space for the caravan to form a buffer for Goenkaji and Mataji's vehicle.

To add to the discomfort of the Dhamma workers, hordes of mosquitoes swarmed in the area, and the showers and restrooms were far away from the vehicles. The crew could take a little comfort in the thought that they would be staying here just for a night. There was a rather nice meadow with a creek running close by but conditions were definitely trying. Nature may be beautiful, but it is not always very hospitable.

The youngest member of the caravan crew had been assisting the cook in serving meals to Goenkaji and Mataji. Today he devised a simple method to catch and release mosquitoes and flies using a cup and a piece of paper. After catching some mosquitoes he would take them out and release them, unhurt. His face shone with happiness at the effectiveness of his non-violent solution.

All these discomforts made the crew members realize just how fortunate it is to have Vipassana centers that offer comfortable accommodation, halls, and cells for quiet, serious meditation. To contribute to the building of secure, comfortable (but not luxurious) places that enable people to meditate with minimal hindrances is truly a greatly meritorious deed.

When Anāthapiṇḍika donated the Jetavana to the Sangha as a dwelling and meditation center, the Buddha approved the donation with these words:

(A proper meditation center) protects one from cold and heat. It keeps out wild animals, reptiles and fleas. Gives shelter during winter and rains.

When sun and wind are fierce it affords protection. One remains at ease and comfortable to practice concentration and Vipassana.

Gifts of viharas (meditation centers) are praised highly by the Buddha. Therefore a wise person, knowing his own welfare, gets comfortable dwellings built for ardent meditators. Such a wise person provides food, water, clothes and a resting place.

In such places, one learns Dhamma to liberate oneself from all misery.

As awareness about Vipassana is spreading in North America and elsewhere in the world, there is an ever-growing demand for courses and for centers. In North America there are waiting lists for most center- and non-center courses. Clearly, more centers are needed to facilitate the spread of Dhamma to more and more suffering people.

During his evening walk, Goenkaji gave instructions on the formation of a new trust for organizing Vipassana courses in the prisons of North America. Now that the effectiveness of Vipassana has been proved in American prisons, and its use becoming more widely accepted, there is a need for an organization that is dedicated to the worthy goal of making Vipassana available at more prisons. Since prisoners are generally not in a position to give donations, financial contributions will be accepted by the new trust from other charitable organizations. And of course, governments and citizens also have a responsibility and incentive to support such benevolent programs. Goenkaji has initiated this policy specifically for the case of North America, where assistant teachers and Dhamma workers often need to travel by air, which is relatively expensive. Preparing course facilities and providing food is also costly. But, as for all courses throughout the world in this tradition, there will be no charge for courses.

Goenkaji made it clear that in keeping with principles he has laid down, he does not want assistant teachers or Dhamma workers involved in this activity to receive any money other than out-of-pocket expenses, for travel costs and the like.

Day 96, July 14, Chicago, IL
Sthitaprajña: From a Distant Dream to a Real Possibility

Once again this morning, Goenkaji had to hurry—to get to the venue of his first talk in the Chicago area, at the Hindu Temple of Greater Chicago.

Initially he had planned to speak in Hindi, but for the benefit of the many people from South India (where Hindi is not well understood), he was asked to speak in English instead.

He told the audience that he was brought up as a devout Hindu. At an early age he learned to recite the Bhagavad Gita by heart. The part of this famous text that appealed to him most was the Gita ideal of *sthitaprajña* (one established in wisdom).

As a young adult, he often gave lectures on Gita and talked a lot about *sthitaprajña—vītarāgabhayakrodhaḥ*, etc. He also recounted his frustrations when he found that despite all his devotion and fervent praying, he was not getting any closer to the ideal. It was only after he took a Vipassana course that he felt that this ideal was within his reach. He had found a path that could make anyone a *sthitaprajña*.

The Enlightened One discovered that impurities are created at the level of sensations—physical, bodily sensations. It is the constant, unconscious reaction to these sensations that generates mental impurities. When one learns to observe the sensations with equanimity, understanding their true nature of impermanence (*anicca*), the accumulated stock of mental impurities starts to evaporate.

It is very important to become aware and alert whenever an impurity (such as anger, hatred, jealousy, fear, greed, or ego) arises. By immediately observing sensations, the impurity loses its strength and becomes weaker and weaker, finally passing away.

If a poisonous snake emerging from a hole is caught before it is completely out, it is not dangerous. But if it is allowed to come out, it becomes dangerous and difficult to contain. Similarly, if one becomes aware of sensations as soon as a mental impurity arise in the mind, there is no danger that the mind will be overpowered.

It was after 2 p.m. when Goenkaji finished his lunch. The caravan had to get to another campground closer to Chicago and then from there to the Field Museum, the venue of his public talk that evening. As soon as his motor home arrived at the campground Goenkaji left for the talk.

Field Museum

At the Field Museum's James Simpson Theater in the evening, Goenkaji emphasized that Vipassana is not a devotional or emotional game. It is not merely an exercise to satisfy intellectual curiosity. It is a serious undertaking to face one's mental impurities and eradicate all forms of suffering. It requires strenuous and continuous work. A ten-day residential Vipassana course is designed to offer a conducive atmosphere for this vital, delicate task.

Goenkaji outlined what is taught in a ten-day Vipassana retreat. The first part of the meditation is awareness of natural breath—a wonderful object of concentration that the Buddha used himself. As well as concentrating the mind, the breath serves also as a tool for exploring the truth about oneself. The meditator simply observes natural respiration, as it is, without adding any verbalization or visualization to it. Just as one does not interfere with the flow of a river when sitting on the bank, simply watching it flow past, a meditator just feels the natural flow of respiration—as it goes in, as it goes out—without doing anything to alter or control that flow.

Though it may seem an easy task, on a ten-day course one learns quickly that it is very difficult. After only a few breaths the mind wanders away from its object. This leads to frustration at the inability of the mind to carry out such an easy task. One has to simply accept that the mind has wandered away, and bring awareness back to the breath. It is a job that requires patience and persistence. The two basic aspects of the practice are to remain with the reality of the present moment and to maintain continuity of that awareness.

By keeping one's awareness within a small area—below the nostrils and above the upper lip—the mind becomes sharper and sharper, and subtler and subtler. And as the mind becomes sharp and subtle it naturally starts to feel the subtle sensations in the body. A gross mind can feel only gross, intense sensations, such as pressure, pain, tension or strong heat. To develop the ability to feel subtle sensations sustained practice is needed. When one is ignorant of the sensations that arise constantly in the body, one keeps on reacting to them—with craving if they are pleasant; with aversion if they are unpleasant. In a Vipassana course students not only learn to feel sensations, but also to maintain equanimity towards them, by understanding their impermanent nature.

Bargain

Whenever Goenkaji gives a talk, the audience listens with rapt attention. As he explains the science of Vipassana and gives an outline of a Vipassana course, the tone of the talk remains quite serious. But the question-and-answer sessions that conclude his talks inevitably bring out Goenkaji's humorous side. With his wise, witty and typically brief answers he makes the audience laugh, even as he clarifies its doubts.

One question that brought peels of laughter was: "Your ten-day Vipassana course sounds very serious to me. Can you suggest something that is shorter, lighter and easier?" Goenkaji replied, "Oh! You have started bargaining! Coming from a business family, I did the same with my teacher." He then went on to explain how he had bargained with his teacher, Sayagyi U Ba Khin. After Sayagyi had explained that to learn Vipassana it was necessary to stay within the confines of a residential facility for a full ten days, Goenkaji asserted that he would stay at the meditation center for a day and then practice for the rest of the period at his home. Patiently, Sayagyi explained that this technique had traditionally been taught in six-week intensive retreats—it had been shortened to ten days to make it more accessible to the busy householders of modern cities. It was found, however, that in anything less than ten days it is not possible for people to get an outline of the technique.

Middle Path

Vipassana is a middle path, between the two extremes—one of denying and torturing oneself, in the false hope of purifying the mind, and the other of indulging heedlessly in sensual pleasures, which leads to the misery of enslavement to mental impurities. The wise seeker avoids these two extremes. Though Vipassana is a serious practice, with the most high-minded spiritual purpose, it does not take away the joy of life. In fact, learning this "art of living" enables one to live actively, responsibly and fruitfully, with greater clarity, peace of mind and joy than before.

Goenkaji also cautioned the audience, pointing out that while Dhamma talks and discourses can help to provide an intellectual appreciation of Dhamma, they are helpful only in so far as they inspire one to take up the practice. Although they can serve as a first step, the real and priceless benefits of Dhamma cannot be had without the experiential wisdom that comes from actual practice.

Day 97, July 15, Chicago, IL
Separation

On this day the crew split up for a day for the first time since the tour began. Goenkaji went to the Arya Samaj site where a one-day course was organized.

Mataji was taken to meet the daughter of the late Dr. Om Prakash. Dr. Om Prakash had been a close friend of Goenkaji for decades, and had served as a Vipassana teacher. He was the doctor who had warned Goenkaji that he risked becoming addicted to morphine if he continued taking it to relieve his migraines, urging him to find an alternative treatment or medication during his travels abroad.

Years later, after Goenkaji became established in Vipassana, a major turning point came in the doctor's life. It happened when he witnessed the passing away of Goenkaji's mother, who had also started practicing Vipassana. When he saw how calmly she faced the great pain of her terminal cancer, how she continued meditating until the very the last moments of her life, and how peacefully she passed away, fully conscious and alert, he was deeply impressed. Then and there he decided to learn Vipassana for himself. Immediately he was able to join a course with Sayagyi U Ba Khin. Due to his great spiritual maturity, on that very course he experienced *nibbāna*, thereby becoming an *ariya*—a saint, a noble one.

Day 98, July 16, Chicago, IL
Essence of Buddha Dhamma

During the morning, Goenkaji and the crew were able to enjoy a short respite from the rigors of tour commitments. Some crew members even took advantage of a nearby lake to take a swim. Goenkaji met with the families that were hosting the Dhamma caravan—cooking meals and looking after their various needs.

In the evening, Goenkaji visited a Myanmar monastery in Chicago. His happy face beamed even brighter than usual at being with people from his motherland. The Myanmar expatriates were greatly pleased and proud to see Sayagyi Goenka taking the precious jewel of Vipassana all around the world, and thereby elevating the image of Myanmar in the eyes of people everywhere.

As the hall became packed, speakers were set up outside the hall for all those who could not get in. In his informal talk, Goenkaji explained how the Buddha taught nothing but *sīla*, *samādhi* and *paññā*.

The Buddha defines his teaching as:
Sabba pāpassa akaraṇaṃ
kusalassa upasampadā
sacittapariyodapanaṃ
etaṃ buddhanasāsanaṃ
Abstain from all evil, unwholesome actions,
Perform only good, wholesome actions,
Purify the mind;
This is the teaching of all Enlightened Ones.

Goenkaji explained how the Buddha talked about *pariyodapanaṃ*—that is, purifying the *totality* of the mind. This is a very important point. It is easy to bring calm to the surface of the mind, but time and again the sleeping volcano of impurities (*anusaya kilesa*) erupts, causing one to react in the same old harmful manner, and continuing the cycle of misery. As long as these *anusaya kilesa*, these sleeping impurities remain, the cycle cannot be broken. The only way to get to the root of the problem, and eradicate these impurities, is to work at the level of physical bodily sensations.

The Buddha said: *Sukhāya, bhikkhave, vedanāya rāgānusayo pahātabbo, dukkhāya vedanāya paṭighānusayo pahātabbo, adukkhamasukhāya vedanāya avijjānusayo pahātabbo.*

Eradicate the latent tendency to craving, by utilizing pleasant sensations (through objective observation of pleasant sensations, understanding their changing nature); eradicate the latent tendency to aversion, utilizing unpleasant sensations, and eradicate the latent tendency to ignorance, utilizing neutral sensations.

A Contradiction in Terms

At the end of the talk, someone asked a question about Buddhist philosophy. Before replying to the question, Goenkaji explained that the term "Buddhist philosophy" is actually a contradiction in terms (though it is widely used for conventional purposes). The Buddha was above all philosophies, above all theories and speculations, because he understood and experienced the truth in its totality. What he taught was not based merely on speculative reasoning. Theories (unsubstantiated hypotheses) are proposed when the truth is not known. The Buddha discovered the truth through his direct experience. What he taught, therefore, was neither a theory nor a philosophy. It is the eternal law of nature that applies whether or not there is a Buddha in the world.

Goenkaji concluded by expressing gratitude to his motherland for the invaluable jewel of Dhamma he received there.

Day 99, July 17, Chicago, IL / Madison, Wisconsin / Chicago, IL

Vipassana Centers

Goenkaji started his day early, as he planned to visit a property that had been offered as a donation for a Vipassana center. Over the past few decades, Goenkaji has inspected hundreds of properties that have been considered as prospective centers. Thus, the local trust could make use of all this experience, as well as Goenkaji's intuitive wisdom of the requirements of a suitable center. It was a two and a half hour drive to the property.

Goenkaji has said:

The establishment of centers marks a new stage in the spread of Vipassana. It is important to understand their significance.

Centers for Vipassana meditation are not clubs designed for the enjoyment of their members. They are not temples in which to perform religious ceremonies. They are not places for socializing or entertainment. They are not communes where members of a sect can live in isolation from the outside world, according to their own particular rules.

Instead, centers are schools, which teach one subject: Dhamma, the art of living. All who come to these centers—whether to meditate or to serve—come to receive this teaching. They must therefore be receptive in their attitude, trying not to impose their ideas, but rather, to understand and to apply the Dhamma that is offered.

After spending some time at the property Goenkaji ate his lunch and then left for Madison, Wisconsin.

Vipassana for Leaders

The title of his evening talk at the University of Wisconsin's Fluno Center was "Benefits of Vipassana for Leaders and Society". Goenkaji spoke to a select audience that included professors, scientists, doctors, accountants, businesspeople and nuns.

Before trying to lead others, said Goenkaji, people in positions of authority, responsibility and influence should first lead themselves along the right path. While everyone needs Vipassana—both leaders and followers—when society's leaders learn and practice it, others will naturally follow them.

Goenkaji explained that the Buddha was a scientist—a super-scientist of spirituality. The Buddha explored the realm of mind and matter completely, experiencing the truth that everything, both material and mental, is ceaselessly arising and passing away. Every particle of matter within the framework of the body is in constant oscillation. Even the matter that makes up inanimate objects, to which no mind is connected, is in constant oscillation: *sabbo loko pakampito*—the entire universe is vibration. Just as the Buddha discovered this truth by exploring the mind-matter phenomenon within, without the aid of any instrument, anyone who practices Vipassana can experience the truth of *anicca* (impermanence) within. The awareness of sensations when coupled with this understanding works to eradicate the accumulated *saṅkhāras* (conditioned impurities), and by this process the mind steadily becomes more and more peaceful. A peaceful, sharp mind is able to grasp situations quickly and clearly. It is able to immediately get to the roots of problems and find effective solutions to them.

A Universal Way to Alleviate Universal Misery

When a person generates anger, hatred, ill-will, lust, fear, or ego, he or she instantly becomes tense and miserable. This is a fixed law of nature—it applies to everyone without exception.

When someone generates anger, it cannot be classified as Christian anger, or a Jewish anger, or Hindu anger, or Buddhist anger, or as male anger, or female anger, or American anger or Russian anger. In the same way, the misery experienced due to that negativity cannot be labeled as Hindu misery or Muslim misery, or Christian misery, or Jewish misery, etc. Misery is universal. And since this disease is universal, the cure for it must also be universal.

The Buddha directed us to concentrate our awareness on the breath, an object of concentration that is universal. Breath cannot be labeled as Hindu breath, or Muslim breath, or Christian breath, or Jewish breath, etc. Similarly, when the mind begins to get purified, the peace and harmony that one experiences cannot be described as Hindu peace, or Muslim peace or Christian peace or Jewish peace etc. Happiness too is universal.

Defiling Impulses

Whenever any impurity arises in the mind it gives rise to a flow of biochemicals that pollute one's entire being. The Pāli word for this intoxicating flow is *āsava*, a word that also refers to the oozing from an ulcer or infected wound. At the time of the Buddha, and even today, in various Indian languages, the word *āshrava (āsava)* is also used to refer to alcoholic drinks. By direct experience, a meditator realizes that all mental impurities such as anger, fear and greed produce a biochemical surge in the body, like the flow of pus from a wound, with an intoxicating effect that prevents one from seeing reality as it is. Since *arahats*—individuals who are totally enlightened or purified—have eradicated all defiling impulses (*āsavas*)—they are referred to as *anāsavo*.

As mentioned earlier, throughout the tour some of Goenkaji's earliest North American students had the opportunity to meet with him for the first time in many years. On this day, several students who had taken Vipassana courses with Goenkaji 25 to 30 years ago came to see him.

Later, Goenkaji met again with the Chicago trust to discuss issues related to establishing a center in the area. In the meeting, he emphasized the importance of putting aside one's personal views when giving Dhamma service.

After Goenkaji ate dinner the caravan started on its way back to Chicago, reaching the night's campsite at 3 a.m.

Day 100, July 18, Chicago, IL / Brighton, Michigan
Healthy Habit

The next stop for the caravan was a Christian retreat center near Detroit, which had been rented by local organizers as a one-day course site, as well as a resting place for the caravan.

When Goenkaji reached the site in Michigan he found a crowd of meditators, mostly young, waiting for him. It was heartening to see so much enthusiasm for Dhamma among the younger generation. Although Goenkaji had been on the road for many hours, he decided to meet immediately with the waiting students. After everyone gathered in a hall, he joined them to answer their questions.

After only one non-center course in the area, local old students were already eager to set up a permanent center. Fortunately for them, they could now take advantage of Goenkaji's personal guidance on this goal.

One student asked whether it was possible to get attached to Vipassana, out of a desire to practice regularly and take repeated meditation courses. "Isn't this a kind of addiction?" Goenkaji explained that if someone is sick, seeing a doctor or taking medication is not done out of attachment or clinging—it is necessary to treat physical illnesses. In the same way, because everyone suffers due to his or her mental impurities, Vipassana is essential for making the mind healthy. Just as eating food and bathing each day are not done out of attachment, neither is the daily practice of Vipassana or taking a ten-day course. The word "addiction" rightly applies only to habits that are physically or mentally harmful or unhealthy. If Vipassana is a habit, then it is certainly a healthy and wholesome habit.

Day 101, July 19, Brighton, Michigan, U.S.A. / Toronto, Canada
A Second Time in Canada

Local old students in Michigan had organized a one-day course to mark Goenkaji's arrival, despite being advised that Goenkaji might not be able to teach any session of the course. Thus, it was to their pleasant surprise that before leaving for Toronto, Goenkaji decided to join the course to give the Anapana instructions.

In the afternoon, the Dhamma caravan crossed into Canada for the second time in the Meditation Now tour of North America.

On the road to Toronto, Goenkaji and Mataji stopped to visit a property that local meditators were considering for a center. They looked carefully over the whole site.

Just before midnight, the caravan reached the quiet and secluded Glen Rouge campground, just outside of Toronto. The site was surrounded by protected forests and a river on one side. Over the next days, the caravan crew would see many playful black squirrels and large, fearless raccoons within the campground. There was also a beautiful trail in the nearby woods for walking or jogging. While some members of the caravan crew might have been tempted by the thought of a swim in the river, none of them ventured in the water—perhaps more because of their busy schedule than the signs advising guests to avoid swimming in the river. On their arrival, the weary crew could think only of getting into bed as soon as they hooked up the motor homes and pitched their tents.

Day 102, July 20, Toronto, Ontario
Auspicious Day

It was a hot and humid day. The crew (most of whom had visited India several times) was reminded of summer in Mumbai. One local meditator joked that he had specially ordered weather that would make the Indian guests feel at home.

There was a festive mood at the Cardinal Carter Academy where a Sangha Dāna was organized for the morning. It was Goenkaji's wish to give Sangha Dāna wherever possible during the tour. More than 50 monks and nuns graced the occasion with their participation, thereby giving faithful householders a wonderful opportunity to earn merits.

After the giving of food, Goenkaji addressed the gathering of lay people in the auditorium. Members of the venerable Sangha were also present on the stage. A senior monk, Ven. Vimala, gave a short talk in which he described Goenkaji as a distinguished master in the 2600-year history of the spread of the Buddha's teaching. While numerous outstanding figures have diffused the wisdom of Dhamma since the time of the Buddha, most of them have been monks. Ven. Vimala praised Goenkaji's accomplishment in taking Dhamma across boundaries of race, religion and nationality, and touching the hearts of hundreds of thousands of people with his gentle and compassionate wisdom.

He expressed a wish to hear more about Goenkaji's efforts to bring Buddha's teaching back to India.

Buddha's Teaching in India: Centuries of Darkness and Misinformation

In his talk, Goenkaji described the great doubt he felt about the Buddha's teaching before taking his first Vipassana retreat. Sayagyi U Ba Khin, his teacher, assured him that the Buddha taught nothing but *sīla*, *samādhi* and *paññā*. In his first course, Goenkaji found that the practice of Vipassana he learned was a rational, scientific and universal teaching that gives results here-and-now. He found nothing to object to in the practical aspect of the Buddha's teaching. Yet, due to his strong conditioning against the Buddha's teaching, he still feared that the theoretical aspect of the teaching might be unacceptable to him.

Goenkaji was once given a translation of the Dhammapada by Bhadant Anand Kausalyayan, a learned scholar-monk from India who stayed in Goenkaji's house whenever he visited Myanmar (Burma). Yet, due to his prejudice against the Buddha, Goenkaji left the book on his table for a full three years without even once opening it. After his first Vipassana course, however, he began to read it, finding himself thrilled by its content. As he studied more and more of the texts of the Tipitaka (firstly in translation and later on in the original Pāli) he discovered that even the theoretical aspect of the Buddha's teaching was stainless. All his doubts had melted away.

For many centuries deep ignorance and tragic misunderstanding have prevailed in India about the country's greatest son, Gotama the Buddha. Now, as the Buddha's teaching returns to India, Goenkaji is trying to dispel some of these unfortunate views.

One of the reasons that India lost the pure Dhamma is that the Buddha was portrayed in Indian literature as an incarnation of Lord Vishnu, thus contradicting a very fundamental aspect of Dhamma, the very liberation of the Buddha. The Buddha declared, *ayaṃ antimā jāti, natthidāni punabbhavoti*—this is my last life, there is no more rebirth for me. Moreover, the Buddha was wrongly regarded to be an incarnation of *māyā-moha* (literally, deception-delusion), the evil qualities of Lord Vishnu.

Another reason for the downfall of the Dhamma in India is that Buddha Dhamma was taken to be a branch of Hinduism, thereby relegating it to a place of secondary importance.

One particularly sad consequence of the loss of the Buddha's teaching from India has been rampant casteism, which has undermined not only the dignity of millions of the so-called lower castes, but also the unity of the nation.

Fortunately, Goenkaji has been able to convince some of India's most eminent spiritual leaders of these past mistakes. Many Hindu leaders now acknowledge such beliefs as false and magnanimously accept the historical truths about the Buddha. Up to now, four Shankaracharyas and many other top Hindu figures have agreed sagaciously not to give currency to these errors. Of course, Goenkaji doesn't believe in quarreling about these or any other matters. In this respect, he always follows the Buddha's advice—

Vivādaṃ bhayato disvā, avivādañca khemato;
samaggā sakhilā hotha, esā buddhānusāsanī

Seeing danger in dispute, security in concord,

Dwell together in amity—this is the teaching of the Buddhas.

Goenkaji expresses his views to others gently, without quarreling. Citing his own example, he points out that no amount of discussion or argument would have convinced him of the benevolent nature of the Buddha's teaching. It was only its practice that convinced him—it is actual practice that yields benefits.

In the conclusion of the talk, he expressed his deep respect and great gratitude towards the Sangha, the order of monks descended from the Buddha, for preserving both the *paṭipatti* (practice) and *pariyatti* (theory) of the Dhamma through the millennia. "If it were not for their efforts, I would never have received these invaluable jewels."

Following his talk, Goenkaji gave personal interviews. When he left the venue he was tired but very happy that he and so many others had been fortunate enough not only to see a large congregation of the Sangha, but also to earn joyful merits by presenting it with *dāna*.

That evening, Goenkaji was interviewed by Ms. Tynette Devaux for Buddha Dharma magazine. He explained to her that even the *word* "Vipassana" had been lost in India after the Buddha's time. After his first meeting with his teacher, Sayagyi U Ba Khin, Goenkaji tried to look up Vipassana, or *Vipaśyanā* (the Sanskrit/Hindi equivalent), in his Hindi and Sanskrit dictionaries. The word was in neither dictionary.

Ms. Devaux wanted to know in what sense could Vipassana be called scientific. Science can be defined as the objective observation of data and the application of this acquired knowledge. Vipassana is the objective observation of the data pertaining to the mind-matter phenomenon at the experiential level. One very basic requirement of any scientific experiment is that it be reproducible. Vipassana has given consistent results over the millennia to anyone and everyone who has practiced it—the results are concrete, tangible, here-and-now.

Goenkaji explained that during a Vipassana course, students carefully observe the five precepts, in order to calm and settle the mind. This is necessary because breaking any of these precepts gives rise to waves of agitation that inhibit the mental concentration required for the proper practice of Vipassana. Without this practice of morality, it is not possible to undertake the delicate task of self-exploration. Goenkaji sometimes explains this with the example of the huge waves that occur in the sea off Mumbai during the monsoon season, bringing oil exploration work to a halt. Later, as one learns to observe the reality within, it becomes very clear that breaking any of the precepts instantly brings suffering upon oneself.

In reference to *anicca*, Goenkaji stressed that it is not a mere philosophy or concept, but rather a basic reality of a existence.

Karma

To a question about karma (*kamma*), he explained that every mental reaction is karma. The karmic seed is the present reaction of the mind, which makes one feel miserable here and now; the karmic fruit of that seed will ripen in the future, bringing with it misery of the same flavor. There is much talk about karma but little understanding—so much discussion about how situations are the result of past karma, yet so little effort to stop the habit of creating new karma in the present moment. The focus of Vipassana is to not generate new karma (*saṅkhāra* or *kamma*). The law of nature is such that as soon as one stops generating new karma, one's old, accumulated karma starts rising up from the depth of the mind to pass away or wash off.

Next, Goenkaji was asked why he doesn't use the word "Buddhism" to describe his teaching. He stated that although he appreciated that the term is commonly used to denote the teaching of the Buddha, he prefers to avoid it because of its sectarian connotation. He is convinced that the Buddha never taught any 'ism.' The Vipassana Research Institute has published a CD-ROM that contains the entire Tipiṭaka (the Buddha's words), amounting to more than 15,000 pages, along with 35,000 pages of commentarial literature. Using the built-in search function provided on the CD, it has been found that in all this vast quantity of literature, neither the word "Buddhist," nor "Buddhism" (*boddha* or *bauddha*) occurs at all. Furthermore, for about 500 years after the Buddha, rival religious traditions in India never referred to the Buddha's teaching as "Buddhism" or "Buddhist." Goenkaji also speaks out of his own conviction, borne of his deep practical experience of Dhamma and his study of the Buddha's words, that the Buddha's teaching is unequivocally universal and non-sectarian. The Buddha was never interested in establishing an organized religion or sect, or teaching dogma or philosophy.

Ms. Devaux also asked Goenkaji about the place and importance of monastic training in Dhamma. Goenkaji said that human life is a precious opportunity to utilize the invaluable

Dhamma. He added that the decision to renounce the household life and take robes should never be taken impulsively—it should be taken only with a mature understanding and serious commitment. Also, to ensure that the Sangha maintains its discipline and purity, novice monks need to be properly trained in Vinaya by senior monks.

Day 103, July 21, Toronto, Ontario
Diversity of Toronto

Large numbers of meditators had the opportunity to meditate in the presence of Goenkaji on his North American tour. On his travels, Goenkaji has taken the Ganges of Dhamma to their doorsteps, and everywhere they took full advantage of it.

Meditators in Toronto had organized a one-day course this day. Goenkaji gave the Vipassana instructions himself, and then answered questions from the students on the course.

In the evening, he gave a public talk at the same venue, which had also hosted the Sangha Dana. So many showed up that more than 200 people (mostly meditators) ended up listening to the talk on simulcasts relayed to two other halls. Remarkably, almost all of Goenkaji's talks throughout the tour drew capacity audiences.

Goenkaji expressed joy at being in a city with such a wonderful multiethnic and multicultural fabric.

You Make Your Future!

In his talk, Goenkaji emphasized that individuals must each take responsibility for their own happiness. A person becomes miserable because he or she generates impurities in their mind. "No outside power has defiled your mind. You are responsible for your defilements. And by eradicating them you can create a happy future for yourself. You make your future!"

Goenkaji exhorted the audience to give the technique of Vipassana a trial for ten days. Of course, at the end of the ten days, one is free to accept or reject the technique.

Goenkaji pointed out that purity of mind is accepted and preached by all religions. The qualities of a pure mind are summarized beautifully in a Hindi verse composed by Goenkaji. It could be translated into English roughly as:

> Let one feel compassion for the miserable,
> Sympathetic joy at the happiness of others;
> Let one be equanimous in adversity,
> In all situations, let one have selfless love for all.

Many expatriate Indians had come to the talk and some of them had kindly given up their places in the main hall for others. In appreciation, Goenkaji met with them at the end of the talk and answered their questions in Hindi. He told them that for centuries, false information had been spread about the Buddha's teaching. India suffered because it lost the teaching. He refuted, one by one, the various misconceptions about the Buddha, such as the mistaken ideas that the Buddha's teaching is pessimistic, that it has made India a weak country, that it was merely a branch of Hinduism, and that the Buddha was an incarnation of Lord Vishnu.

Goenkaji then met with the Sri Lankan Consular General who expressed his appreciation for Goenkaji's work and promised to take a ten-day course.

Day 104, July 22, Toronto, Ontario

Diversity of Toronto

This morning was reserved for media interviews. First, Goenkaji was interviewed for a national public television (PBS) documentary. Goenkaji stressed that tolerance is the essence of every religion. Those that feel that they are religious just because they visit a temple, church, mosque or synagogue are deluding themselves. It is not by the mere performance of rites and rituals that a person becomes religious. It is tolerance, love and compassion that make one truly holy and religious.

Vipassana is a way to make oneself truly holy. It is a process of self-correction through self-examination.

Ageing

To a question about ageing, Goenkaji answered that although old age is certainly a misery, old age by itself cannot make one unhappy. If people can couple the wealth of their life experience with wisdom, old age can be the golden years of their life—a period where they can look at things with serenity and deep understanding. Such a happy old age is also a great source of joy for others.

"I am ageing happily," announced Goenkaji. "There is decay, every moment; birth and death, every moment. But I remember how miserable I was when I was 30. Now almost 50 years later I find myself a lot happier and healthier. Old age suits me well. I have more wisdom and I have so much happiness. I travel around the world to distribute happiness. I am meeting old students who are serious practitioners of Vipassana and I also meet people who have never heard the word Vipassana."

He added, "The more happiness I distribute, the happier I get!"

Material possessions are ephemeral, so any happiness derived from material pleasures is inherently fragile. In contrast, the happiness that comes from wisdom is substantial and lasting.

In view of Vipassana's emphasis on the reality within, Goenkaji was asked, how important are the outward realities of the world? Goenkaji confirmed that it is important to be aware of outer realities when leading a worldly life. But that is only half of the truth—the other, more important part of the picture is the reality inside. To be aware of the totality of the truth, one must be aware of the truth both inside and outside.

Death and Dying

"One can learn the art of dying only when one has learned the art of living," answered Goenkaji when asked about death and dying. Every moment there is death, and every moment there is birth. The flow of mind and matter continues from moment to moment. By learning this, one readies oneself for the flow across the boundary of conventional death, from one existence to another. Worrying about the future results in fear. The only way to be ready for the future is to be ready for the present.

Real Strength

Goenkaji was asked to define what real strength is in this life. He answered that there is no strength in life like the strength of a pure mind. Nothing can shake a pure mind. A truly powerful person is one who is not disturbed by the things around him or her.

Success

The interviewer asked Goenkaji to give his definition of success. Goenkaji revealed that before learning Vipassana he had thought that success was being better than others. "But after Vipassana I discovered that true success is being happy. I consider myself successful when I see how much I have come out of misery; and also when I serve and see so much change in others." He also noted a big change in the way he gave donations. Before Vipassana, it was with the intention of advancing his reputation; after Vipassana, he began giving donations out of compassion; in order to help others. Donations are far more fruitful when they are given out of selfless love and compassion.

Yours to Discover: Ontario and Vipassana

After the PBS television interview, a journalist and a photographer from the Toronto Star, the largest newspaper in Canada, arrived at the campground to interview Goenkaji. The license plates of all vehicles in the province of Ontario carry the slogan, "Yours to Discover", a phrase that could serve as a translation of *ehi passiko*—one of the key characteristics of Dhamma, which means "come and see." Dhamma invites people to come and see. As Goenkaji keeps saying in his public talks—come and try it for ten days. When the journalist was told about this correlation, he was quite amused and impressed, and even made mention of it in his article.

In the evening, Goenkaji met with the Toronto trust and others who came to the campground from surrounding areas.

Day 105, July 23, Toronto / Ottawa, Ontario
Secluded Campgrounds

Since the arrival of the Dhamma caravan here rain fell unabated, and the weather had cooled. The caravan settled in an isolated corner of the campground, surrounded by woods with a river flowing by. All were pleased by the privacy and atmosphere.

In the morning, the caravan left for Ottawa, the capital of Canada. By the time it had reached its campground, evening had fallen. A large section of the park had been reserved for the tour vehicles, and the caravan found itself in a beautiful secluded area amidst gentle, pleasant woods. Local meditators had erected a large tent within the campground for meditation and meetings. A canopy was put up too, to create a makeshift dining room.

Many meditators awaited the caravan. Goenkaji decided to meet them immediately on arrival. After spending some time with them, he took a walk with the local teacher. He then met with Ron Graham, one of his oldest Canadian students, to prepare for the following day's meeting with the Prime Minister of Canada.

Day 106, July 24, Ottawa
The Wheel of Dhamma Rotates—Meeting with the Prime Minister of Canada

It was on this auspicious full moon day of the year, some 2,600 years ago, that the Buddha threw open the doors to liberation by illumining the path out of suffering. The "teacher of gods and men" had proclaimed the Middle Path (*majjhimā paṭipadā*). Now, after many long centuries of darkness, the glorious teaching is making a comeback.

On this day Goenkaji met for an extended private discussion with Mr. Jean Chretien, the Prime Minister of Canada.

The Prime Minister devoted a full 30 minutes to the meeting, without any interruptions for phone calls or disturbances from his staff. Thus, the two leaders were able to converse in a quiet atmosphere on a wide range of topics.

Mr. Chretien expressed pride in Canada's liberal, tolerant and multicultural society. Since a long time, Canada has welcomed migrants from all over the world with open arms. This is akin to the Vipassana community, which is similarly diverse in its make-up. Goenkaji talked about the potential of Vipassana in bringing about peace and harmony in today's society. He explained the practical, pragmatic and non-sectarian nature of the practice, referring to the utilization of Vipassana by state governments in India.

The Prime Minister expressed his concern over the First Nations (descendants of Canada's native inhabitants). Goenkaji responded by pointing out how New Zealand's Maori community is taking advantage of the power of Vipassana. Maori people are using the training they receive in Vipassana courses to help them break away from alcohol and drug dependence, a serious problem common to many communities of native peoples around the world. A unique feature of Vipassana is that it helps such people without eroding their original culture. Goenkaji has often described this process using the simile of milk and sugar, explaining that Vipassana always sweetens the culture to which it is added, without disrupting it.

This meeting between a master of the art of statesmanship and a master of the art of peaceful living was truly significant. Goenkaji, who has practiced Vipassana for more than 40 years, told Mr. Chretien, who has been an MP for close to 40 years, about Ashoka—the great Indian emperor who promoted the practice of Vipassana meditation throughout his vast empire, which, by today's borders, extended from Afghanistan to Bangladesh. Within this empire, people of many different religious sects lived together peacefully, just as the multicultural population of Canada does today.

After returning from his meeting with the Prime Minister, Goenkaji was interviewed for the local news TV channel.

Later on he met two serious old students who had flown in from Israel to meet him and to seek his blessing for their forthcoming marriage.

An expatriate Indian couple came to pay respect to their teacher on the occasion of *Guru Purnima*, literally, "the full moon day of the teacher," so-named because the Buddha gave his first discourse—the *Dhammacakkappavattana sutta* (Discourse on the Turning of the Wheel of Dhamma) on this very day of the year in Sarnath.

In the evening, Goenkaji gave a public talk at Carleton University. Again, as the hall started filling up, many meditators gave up their seats to those who had not heard Goenkaji before. Fortunately, a simulcast was arranged in another hall, so that these old students could listen to their teacher on this auspicious day.

Goenkaji explained that the essence of Dhamma is the Four Noble Truths. The Buddha taught what misery is, what the cause of misery is, what the cessation of misery is, and what the way leading to the cessation of misery is.

The Ambassador of Myanmar and the High Commissioner of Sri Lanka attended the discourse, and after the talk they met with Goenkaji and expressed their appreciation for the historic work he is doing in distributing the treasure of the Theravadin countries to the rest of the world.

Day 107, July 25, Ottawa / Dhamma Suttama, Quebec
Into French-speaking Canada

In the morning, Goenkaji met with a *bhikkhu* who had traveled from Toronto to see him. As a result, the caravan's departure from Ottawa was delayed.

Soon after setting out the vehicles crossed into Quebec, the French-speaking province of Canada. So far throughout its long journey, the Dhamma caravan had rarely been stuck in traffic jams, but today's crossing of Montreal proved to be very slow. To minimize delays, the caravan was advised to take an alternate route to *Dhamma Suttama*, Quebec's Vipassana center. For the crew members, the trip turned out to be a real treat, as their weariness was washed away by the beauty of the Quebec countryside and the pleasant cool of the evening.

When the caravan arrived at *Dhamma Suttama*, set amidst hilly country, a little daylight still remained, and the mooing of cows could be heard from a paddock across the road from the center. Local meditators had cleared a small area in the woods on the center property to make a place for the caravan. In the future this clearing will be used as a parking lot.

Day 108, July 26, Dhamma Suttama, Quebec / Montreal / Dhamma Suttama, Quebec

First Course in North America

When Goenkaji traveled to the West for the first time on his Dhamma mission, his first stop in the Americas was Montreal. Montreal holds the honor of being the first place in the Americas to host a ten-day Vipassana course in this tradition.

After giving the Vipassana instructions in the morning at the one-day course at *Dhamma Suttama*, Goenkaji had to go to Montreal, a trip of almost two hours by car. Thus far on the tour, the peace-loving citizens of Canada had thronged to Goenkaji's public talks. Montreal was no exception. As usual, many meditators here at the University of Quebec gave up their places in the hall to enable others to listen and watch Goenkaji.

Heavy traffic prevented a bus load of old students from *Dhamma Suttama* from arriving in time for the talk. Though somewhat disappointed, they were gladdened to know that their places were all taken by people who were hearing Goenkaji's Dhamma message for the first time. Those in the bus would get the opportunity to consult Goenkaji about their practice back at the center.

Since French is the first language of a majority of people in Quebec, Goenkaji's talk was translated into French by Roger Gosselin, who along with his Iranian wife Mersedeh, was among the earliest assistant teachers appointed by Goenkaji.

Goenkaji explained the practice that participants in a ten-day Vipassana course undergo. He emphasized that for the most part, students are expected to meditate in a sitting posture, keeping their back and neck straight, so that the mind remains fully alert and attentive.

Wandering Teacher, Focused Mind

As he often does in his Dhamma talks, Goenkaji describes how beginning meditators quickly come to the surprising realization that they cannot muster enough concentration to accomplish the seemingly easy task of watching their breath flow in and out of their noses. After only a few breaths the mind escapes their awareness. "What a fickle, fleeting, wandering mind!" they think to themselves.

While Goenkaji has wandered far and wide during this and other tours, he has always remained steadfastly focused on a single objective—the spread of pure Dhamma for the benefit and welfare of many—just as the first bhikkhus who learned Dhamma from the Enlightened One were exhorted by him to wander far and wide to spread the teaching.

As the mind becomes concentrated, it is able to start feeling the different sensations that arise constantly in the body. This is the first basic aspect of Vipassana—experiencing, or being aware of sensations. The second basic aspect is maintaining equanimity to the sensations that are experienced. Feeling and understanding the impermanent nature of bodily sensations helps in maintaining equanimity. At the same time, as one's equanimity develops, the impermanent nature of all sensations becomes more and more apparent.

Distributing Peace

Goenkaji was asked why he is touring North America. He replied that because Vipassana has given him so much peace and happiness, he wants to share these gifts with as many people as possible. This is one of the basic qualities of Dhamma: *ehi passiko*.

Women in Dhamma

To a question as to whether there are any female teachers in Dhamma, Goenkaji said that it makes no difference whether someone is a man or a woman. Dhamma is for all. There are many female teachers in Vipassana, he said, and pointing to Mataji, he added that one was sitting next to him.

There are many examples in the Tipiṭaka (the words of the Buddha) of female householders and bhikkhunis who not only achieved the highest meditative attainments but also taught Dhamma to others— to men as well as laywomen. A shining example of this was the *bhikkhuṇi* Dhammadinnā. One day, her former husband, Visākha (not to be confused with Visākhā, the foremost female lay disciple of the Buddha), approached her and put various questions about Dhamma to her. One by one, Dhammadinnā confidently answered the highly technical and profound questions she was asked. Then, after Visākha asked her about still higher truths, the *bhikkhuṇi* told him that even if she were to answer his question, he would not understand her because he had not experienced higher stages of *nibbāna*. Later Visākha approached the Buddha and narrated the incident. On hearing what happened, the Buddha praised Dhammadinnā as a person of great wisdom, adding that she had answered the questions exactly as he, the Buddha, would have done.

Be a Good Human Being First

In his talks, Goenkaji often talks of the importance of becoming a good human being. He asks, "If one is not a good human being, how can one be a good Christian or a good Muslim or a good Hindu or a good Jew? Vipassana teaches one to be a good human being, and thereby a good Christian, a good Muslim, a good Hindu or a good Jew, as the case may be."

The Best Advertising is Word of Mouth

In answering a question, Goenkaji remarked that Vipassana had so far spread mostly through word of mouth. When people benefit from the technique, they naturally wish to see others learn it.

To another question, on whether the practice of Vipassana can lead to the attainment of supernatural powers and the ability to perform miracles, Goenkaji replied that the greatest miracle is liberation from suffering. The Buddha distinguished between mundane, or ordinary, *abhiññās*, and supramundane *abhiññās*. Ordinary miracles include levitation, walking on water, divine sight, divine hearing and mind reading. The Buddha clearly stated that all such powers are worthless because they cannot make a person happy. The only true miracle is the supramundane achievement of eradicating mental impurities and thereby freeing oneself from misery.

The same person asked Goenkaji whether learning Vipassana could help one to communicate with guardian angels. The succinct reply was, "Learn to communicate with yourself first, for that is more important!"

Day 109, July 27, Dhamma Suttama, Quebec
In the Service of Dhamma

The caravan crew had hoped that Goenkaji would be able to take some time out here at the center to tackle some of his writing work and correspondence, and perhaps to rest a little. But again, the morning turned out to be a busy one. There were many people who wanted to see Goenkaji. The private meetings that he began in the morning continued until past lunchtime. Then, just as he finished his last interview, he received an overseas phone call. As it turned out, he was not able to rest until 4 p.m.

Goenkaji sets an example of always being available for the service of Dhamma. Today was a good example of this attitude. In the evening, Goenkaji decided to go and meditate with the old students who had gathered for the day at *Dhamma Suttama*, and offer them a brief talk on Dhamma service.

In his talk he spoke of how he had meditated under the guidance of Sayagyi U Ba Khin for 14 years before being appointed and authorized to teach on his own. During those years he would go to the center often, serving in whatever capacity he could. When his respected teacher wished him to start teaching Vipassana, Goenkaji humbly expressed doubts about his ability. Sayagyi reassured him by reminding him that he had already given an enormous amount service in various capacities, for example, as an interpreter for Hindi-speaking students. Sayagyi pointed out that all this service had earned him a good stock of *pāramis*, which would give him immense strength in his future service. As Goenkaji started to teach, he found this to be very true.

Service is Essential for Progress in Dhamma

Goenkaji explained that the service one gives at Vipassana courses or centers clearly helps one's progress on the path. Volition to give Dhamma service arises naturally as one progresses in Dhamma. Without Dhamma service, one's practice inevitably remains weak.

Dhamma service affords Vipassana students an opportunity to apply and practice, in a conducive environment, all the Dhamma skills they have learned and developed while sitting Vipassana courses. For example, students can train themselves to serve without ego and to deal with students and co-workers with love and compassion. Furthermore, servers get to spend time with other meditators, thereby gaining inspiration and experience, and enjoying the blessing of good Dhamma company. Another benefit is that serving provides an opportunity to clarify one's doubts about Dhamma. Quite naturally, one's understanding of Dhamma deepens with experience in service. And perhaps the greatest reward of Dhamma service is the sympathetic joy that arises from seeing so many students meditating seriously, to liberate themselves from all misery. It is immensely satisfying to see the faces of those who have joined a course transformed in ten days from darkness and gloom to brightness and joy.

A few years ago, Goenkaji said that, ideally, Vipassana students should sit for at least one ten-day course a year, and serve one or more courses too. In connection to this, it is worth noting that old students can serve on courses on a part-time basis, or come just for a day or two to help with center maintenance. Other notable opportunities for service include hosting group sittings, and organizing or managing one-day courses. There are many ways to serve!

Day 110, July 28, Dhamma Suttama, Quebec
Expanding Center

The one-day course at *Dhamma Suttama* offered meditators in Quebec one more opportunity to come to the center. Due to limited accommodation at the center many of them drove many hours to make a day trip.

Goenkaji's morning again started with a flurry of interview appointments. Firstly, two journalists from a major French-language daily in Quebec came to interview Goenkaji. Goenkaji then went to answer questions from students in the tent that was erected to serve as a large meditation hall during his visit.

In the evening, he again granted private interviews before going to the temporary meditation hall for talks with local trustees and assistant teachers. He emphasized the need to expand the capacity of the center to meet growing demand. He looked around the property and gave guidance on how the center could be expanded.

Day 111, July 29, Dhamma Suttama, Quebec / Boston, MA
Back in the U.S.

This was the end of the second Canadian stage of the tour. The Dhamma caravan left *Dhamma Suttama*, making its way through the winding roads of the Quebec countryside, dotted with gentle hills, rolling meadows and quaint little towns.

Less than half an hour after setting off, the caravan passed through a small border crossing into the U.S. It continued its way through the green mountains of Vermont, reaching the campground in Littleton by the evening. This had been the last day of road travel for the tour.

Day 112, July 30, Boston, MA.

Caravan Crew

As there was no scheduled event this morning, Goenkaji decided to use the time to meet with some of the volunteers serving as part of the caravan crew. Despite traveling with Goenkaji for many weeks, some of them had not sought a single interview with their teacher. Today, the servers were able to meet with their teacher individually, express their gratitude to him in person and seek guidance on their practice. Goenkaji expressed joy and appreciation for the selfless service they had rendered.

John Hancock Center

Throughout the tour Goenkaji had talked to many business people, and today, again, at the John Hancock Center he offered a Dhamma discourse to an audience of invited businesspeople.

Goenkaji explained that as people achieve worldly success and accumulate material wealth, they tend to develop increasing attachment to their gains. The more material comforts and sensual pleasures they experience, the greater their anxiety about preserving them. As a result, they are beset by tension and fear. He then went on to narrate his own experiences as a businessman, and how Vipassana changed his life.

Charity

When people earn money they tend to develop ego. And as long as they have ego, they cannot have any real peace of mind. Although householders need to earn money, they should be careful that in doing so they do not inflate their ego. Good meditators understand that any money that they earn should be used not only to support themselves and their dependents, but also to help other people. They should share whatever they earn. This is the proper attitude for those who wish to dissolve their ego.

The amount of a donation should always be decided according to one's means. Whether the amount is more or less is not that important—as long as the donation is given with a pure volition, that is, without expecting anything in return for the gift. If there is any expectation of receiving something in return for one's donation, then the giving is impure.

Only charity that is practiced with the volition to serve others, to see others emerge from their misery, can genuinely help one to move along the path to real peace.

The more money that businesspeople earn, the more important it is for them to put aside part of their earnings for the benefit of society.

Spiritual Attainments

At the end of the talk, Goenkaji's was asked about his spiritual attainments. He replied that whatever real attainments he might have, they should be reflected in his life. If one's so-called spiritual attainments do not translate into real, noble, upstanding behavior in life, then they are useless.

Anyone who is seeking after particular meditative experiences, rather than checking whether their meditation has made them happier and more peaceful, is missing the entire purpose of Vipassana. Attachment to "special" meditation experiences only serves to reinforce one's ego, thereby increasing unhappiness instead of reducing it.

Day 113, July 31, Boston, MA.
Talk at MIT

Again this morning, Goenkaji spent time with the members of the caravan crew that had served him during the tour.

In the evening, he spoke at the Kresge Auditorium at the Massachusetts Institute of Technology (MIT). Goenkaji expressed the joy he felt to be speaking in a great city that is blessed with so many world-renowned educational institutions. In his talk, he explained that Vipassana is a scientific way of understanding oneself.

At the end of the talk he was asked about miracles and meditation. The greatest miracle is when a suffering person is liberated from that suffering, he answered. All other miracles are irrelevant.

Another question concerned modern scientific discoveries and the Buddha's insights into material phenomena. Goenkaji said that the Buddha undoubtedly knew a great deal more than he actually taught or talked about. The Buddha discovered an enormity of truths in the course of his exhaustive exploration of the mind and matter phenomenon. Yet, he spoke only about what is relevant to the task of achieving liberation from suffering. Once, while traveling through a vast jungle with a group of monks, the Buddha took up a handful of leaves in his hand and explained that in comparison to all that he knew and understood, what he spoke of and taught was like the few leaves in his hand when measured against all the leaves of the vast jungle. He taught only that which is necessary and relevant for liberation.

Goenkaji was also asked why he says so little about advanced stages of meditation in his public talks and even in his ten-day courses. Goenkaji answered that theory and practice should always go hand in hand. Intellectual knowledge about the so-called higher stages of meditation would be useless to those who have not experienced them and could become obstacle to progress. Goenkaji explained that Dhamma is like a great ocean that becomes gradually deeper as one moves further and further from the shore. The Dhamma becomes increasingly more deep and profound as one progresses on the path of Dhamma.

After the talk, the caravan drove to *Dhamma Dharā*, the Vipassana center in Shelburne Falls, arriving there after 1 a.m.

Day 114, August 1, Dhamma Dharā, Shelburne Falls, MA.
VMC: 20 Years of Service

Amongst local meditators, *Dhamma Dharā*, the Vipassana center in Shelburne Falls, is popularly known as VMC (Vipassana Meditation Center). Since it was established as the first center in North America, it has been serving this corner of the globe for 20 years. Old students in the region, especially those who have volunteered their Dhamma services over the past two decades, were greatly pleased that Goenkaji would be visiting the center on its 20th anniversary. After the purchase of the property, many young and enthusiastic Vipassana students had offered their time and skills to build the center, and some of these were present during Goenkaji's current visit.

In the morning, Goenkaji led the concluding *mettā* meditation session of the 30-day course being held at the center. Then from 12 noon he met with many of the students from the course.

In the evening, he meditated in the central meditation cell of the beautiful and quiet pagoda—one of the oldest in the tradition—providing a precious opportunity for many to meditate in the presence of their teacher. Despite the stifling heat and busy schedule of the day, all felt refreshed.

One old student who participated in the sitting—someone who had given a lot of service at VMC over the years—was in the advanced stage of terminal cancer. He and his meditator wife had earlier told Goenkaji that their Vipassana practice enabled them to face death's approach with equanimity and even joy. Goenkaji was happy to see such a glittering example of Dhamma courage and strength.

The Crew Disperses

Since the center was filled to capacity, the caravan crew members were forced to disperse, as they had to be accommodated in different places. A number of them stayed in the homes of old students living close to the center.

Some of the crew tried to finish off assorted tasks before the end of the tour, while others enjoyed a well-earned rest or took advantage of Goenkaji's presence to meditate as much as possible at the center.

Day 115, August 2, VMC, Shelburne Falls, MA.

Meeting More Meditators

Goenkaji spent most of the day meeting meditators and answering their questions. He also took time to walk around the property with local teachers. It was a nostalgic walk for Goenkaji and Mataji as they remembered the various stages of development of this first center in the West.

At noon, Goenkaji held a question-and-answer session in the Dhamma hall, which was filled with eager old students.

In the evening, he met with the center trustees and senior Dhamma workers, along with local assistant teachers. He stressed the point that since assistant teachers and teachers are highly experienced in Dhamma work, trustees should take care to listen closely to their advice. He asked assistant teachers and teachers to remain actively involved in all the important decisions made at centers, especially those involving the expenditure of large sums of money.

Day 116, August 3, VMC, Shelburne Falls, MA.

One-Day Course

Meditators arrived from all over the continent for the opportunity to meditate with Goenkaji in a one-day course at VMC. Goenkaji gave the Anapana and Vipassana instructions to the students in person.

In the evening, Goenkaji met again with meditators.

Packing Up

Mataji was busy packing for their departure to New York the next day. The motor homes would not be used on this final leg of the North American section of the tour, as Goenkaji and Mataji were to stay in an apartment. As Mataji packed, Goenkaji continued with his work. By the day's end, most of the packing was done.

Some volunteers took care of packing the kitchen equipment, books and other items that the caravan had carried throughout the tour.

Some of the servers who had been part of the caravan crew earlier in the tour returned to *Dhamma Dharā*. They were happy to reunite with the old students who had taken over their duties.

Day 117, August 4, VMC, Shelburne Falls, MA.
Remembering Goenkaji
In the evening, Goenkaji gave a talk in the Helen Hills Chapel at Smith College in Northampton. On his previous visit to the U.S. two years earlier Goenkaji had given a talk at the same venue.

Goenkaji spoke about how he came to Dhamma. He talked of the initial doubts he had felt about the Buddha's teaching and how he became gradually convinced of its truth and value through the verification of his own practice and the clear, straightforward explanations provided in the words of the Buddha.

There were many questions after the talk. One person asked Goenkaji how he would like to be remembered by future generations. He replied, "Why remember me? Remember the teaching of the Buddha. That is all that matters."

After the talk, Goenkaji returned to the parking lot where his motor home was parked. Inside he ate his dinner—the last meal he would eat in the motor home. It was the last time the two main vehicles of the caravan would be together. Most of the other vehicles had already split off. The motor home that served as the kitchen was then driven back to *Dhamma Dharā*.

It was late when Goenkaji's motor home began its journey to New York, reaching Manhattan around 3 a.m. By the time all necessary items were removed from the motor home and the apartment was properly set up it was almost 4 a.m. Goenkaji's "car house" as he called his motor home, left immediately for *Dhamma Dharā*.

Day 118, August 5, Manhattan / Queens / Manhattan, New York
Monkey Mind
In the evening, Goenkaji gave a public talk in the Sheraton Hotel, Queens, an area of New York City that is home to a vibrant community of expatriate Chinese meditators. A talk had been organized at the same venue during Goenkaji's previous

visit in the year 2000. Tonight's talk was translated into Mandarin.

In ten-day Vipassana courses Goenkaji talks about how extraordinarily fickle the mind is, incessantly leaping from one object to another like a restless monkey swinging from one branch of a tree to another. Tonight again, Goenkaji explained how we could train the "monkey mind" through the awareness of our breath.

By simply keeping one's attention within the small area below the nostrils and above the upper lip, the mind becomes progressively sharper, to the point where it starts to feel a subtler level of reality—the physical sensations that manifest in this area. Working further, the meditator learns to become aware of sensations throughout the body.

At the end of the talk Goenkaji answered questions from the audience and then met with groups of meditators and their relatives and friends.

Day 119, August 6, Manhattan, New York
Exhibition Gallery of the Global Pagoda

The remaining members of the crew had hoped that today's schedule would be relatively unhurried, but Goenkaji had other plans.

In the morning, Goenkaji set out for an "educational tour" of the Museum of Natural History to see how advanced multimedia technology is being used to present information at modern museums exhibition facilities.

The exhibition gallery at the Global Pagoda, which is currently under construction, will present historical information about the Buddha and his teaching. One of the central purposes of the project is to help dispel the widespread misunderstandings in India about the Buddha and his teaching. Goenkaji is seeking effective ways to realize this objective. He has already developed an outline of the content to be presented in the gallery, and now he is looking to find the most effective ways to present this precious information to people.

During his visit, he was able to observe a variety of dioramas, and learn more about current interactive methods of education.

Next, Goenkaji decided to visit the Ellis Island Museum of Immigration, which provides an excellent example of how serious historical subject matter can be effectively presented. Again, Goenkaji was interested to see novel ways of presenting information.

Due to many centuries of false propaganda, the Buddha's teaching is seen in a negative light by many Indians. The Global Pagoda is intended to serve as a focus point for correcting this misinformation.

Goenkaji did not return to his apartment until late in the evening.

Day 120, August 7, New York, USA / London, U.K. / Brussels, Belgium

India's Role in the Spread of Dhamma

On this day Goenkaji took another opportunity to give a Sangha Dāna, this time at the New York Vihara, which was kindly made available by Ven. Piyatissa Mahathera. Despite the fact that it was a working day and that the event was arranged on short notice, a large number of local Vipassana students took the opportunity to visit the vihara and serve the gathering of virtuous monks. The highly respected scholar-monk Ven. Bodhi Mahathera (Bhikkhu Bodhi) had also consented kindly to be present at the Sangha Dāna. Goenkaji, Mataji and so many Vipassana meditators felt great joy at the chance to serve such a distinguished gathering of monks.

The ambassadors of the permanent commissions of Myanmar and Sri Lanka also took the opportunity to come and join in this meritorious deed.

After some chanting of *parittas*, Bhikkhu Bodhi gave a short address to the gathering. He said that humankind is currently facing two extremist evils. The first of these, rampant materialism, is pushing mankind towards hedonism. Corporate greed and excessive individualism are widening the gap between rich and poor, thereby undermining the stability of human society.

The second evil, religious fundamentalism, is eroding the values of tolerance and mutual understanding, and leading to fanatical outbursts of violence that heartlessly snatch away the lives of many innocent people.

Bhikkhu Bodhi stressed that the message of the Buddha-Dhamma is badly needed to offer a sane alternative to these damaging extremes. He expressed his appreciation for the work of Goenkaji, whose style of teaching is well suited to the people of the modern world, particularly those who do not already have devotion towards the Buddha. Goenkaji's emphasis on experiential wisdom strikes a chord with today's scientific and rationalist generations. This approach has enabled Goenkaji to take the Buddha's teaching throughout the world, to people of all religious and ethnic backgrounds.

"Most importantly," concluded Bhikkhu Bodhi, "Goenkaji's efforts and success in the revival of the Buddha's teaching in India are extremely valuable. The world looks upon India as the home of spirituality. For the followers of the Buddha, India has even more significance. Unfortunately, in the last millennium India suffered both in the field of spirituality and material progress. Goenkaji's early success in bringing Vipassana to all sections of the Indian society is a good sign. It is important for India to become strong in Dhamma so as to be the driving force behind the revival of the Buddha Dhamma around the world."

Goenkaji spoke after Bhikkhu Bodhi. He thanked the Sangha for giving him the opportunity to serve them and he expressed gratitude to the Sangha for preserving *pariyatti* and *paṭipatti*, the theory and practice of Dhamma. In addition, he echoed Bhikkhu Bodhi's sentiments on the relevance of the Buddha's teaching in today's world. Immediately after the Sangha Dāna, Goenkaji and Mataji were driven to the airport. Only a few of the caravan crew were there to bid them goodbye. They flew out in the early evening for Brussels via London.

Day 121, August 8, Dhamma Pajjota, Belgium
Arrival in Europe

Goenkaji and Mataji had agreed to stop in Europe on the way back to India from America. They arrived at Brussels airport on the morning of August 8 and were taken to *Dhamma Pajjota*.

Torrential rain the day before had failed to dampen the enthusiasm of Dhamma workers who had arrived at the Belgian center from all over Europe. As Goenkaji's car drove in, they could be seen, busily engaged in tasks such as painting the road-front building and cleaning the grounds.

Goenkaji's residence was on the top floor of the center's main, three-storey building, which includes accommodation for students as well as assistant teachers. Due a knee injury he suffered several years ago, Goenkaji has difficulty climbing steps, so whenever he needs to stay in a building where there is no elevator, a stair-lift is temporarily installed. At *Dhamma Pajjota*, a Scalamobile (a chair operated by another person that lifts or lowers the carried person one step at a time) was hired for Goenkaji. A local assistant teacher took on the responsibility of operating the Scalamobile.

Large tents had been erected at the center to serve as dormitory-style accommodation for the students arriving from around Europe and beyond.

There were no formal engagements on this day.

Day 122, August 9, Dhamma Pajjota, Belgium
Violence and Strict Disciplinary Action

On the morning of August 9, Goenkaji was scheduled to give a press conference. Print media and television reporters arrived in a stream at the center for the event. When asked about the purpose of his tour, Goenkaji explained that it was to take the message of Dhamma to the maximum number of people. He is also able to meet and encourage his students in different parts of the world, but more importantly, such tours are an opportunity to draw the interest of people who have not heard about Vipassana, through public talks and media interviews.

He said that he was happy to see that the Buddha's pragmatic teaching is gaining increasing acceptance in the West. He emphasized that peace on earth can be achieved only if each of us, make our minds healthy.

One journalist asked about the difference between violence and strict disciplinary action. Goenkaji pointed out that when necessary, it is okay to take very strong physical or vocal action, if it is done with the base of a compassionate mind. If there is no compassion in the mind, however, one's actions are bound to become violent and ineffective.

Not 'My' Centers

One question put to Goenkaji used the expression "your centers." Quickly, Goenkaji corrected the reporter. "Vipassana centers are not my centers. They belong to all Vipassana meditators. They build them and run them as per the principles of Vipassana in this tradition."

Infirm Body, Firm Mind

Another questioner quizzed Goenkaji about his own advanced age and eventual death. The body is bound to become old, decayed and frail, replied Goenkaji. It is bound to be afflicted by various diseases. If one practices Vipassana, however, the mind remains healthy and at peace, regardless of physical traumas. He added that, "When one lives in the present moment, one becomes fearless."

In the television interview he exhorted viewers to come and give Vipassana a try. "Don't be afraid. Come and see for yourself. It is not a cult or a 'foreign' faith. It is a simple mental exercise that keeps the mind healthy and happy."

Will Vipassana Last?

One reporter asked him whether he is worried that Vipassana will not last very long after he passes away. Goenkaji answered that he has no such worries. As long as the purity of the technique is maintained and Vipassana centers operate on a non-commercial basis, Vipassana will certainly last. Whenever there is any doubt about the purity, the Buddha's words are available to serve as a beacon. The practice fully accords with the words of the Buddha.

In the evening, Goenkaji gave a public talk in the nearby city of Hasselt, at the cultural center there. The talk, entitled "Inner Peace for a Better World," and translated into Dutch by a meditator, drew a capacity crowd.

Goenkaji said that while the word "Vipassana" is new to most parts of the world, people are now slowly coming to understand that it refers to a simple, scientific, non-sectarian and beneficial practice that delivers results here and now, and involves no conversion from one organized religion to another organized religion.

As usual the talk was followed by a lively question-and-answer session.

Day 123, August 10, Dhamma Pajjota, Belgium
Largest Ever Course Outside of South Asia

A one-day course was scheduled for this day at *Dhamma Pajjota*. A huge tent erected to serve as the meditation hall was designed to accommodate approximately 800 students from 20 different countries. It would be the largest course ever held outside of South Asia. Goenkaji came to the hall to give the Vipassana instructions.

A film crew from Reuters filmed the day's events, recording various scenes of the historic course from different vantage points of the site. Goenkaji gave an interview to the film crew, as did the conducting teacher and four students.

The Reuters report was broadcast later in the day in a three-minute slot during the 7 p.m. news program of the national Belgian TV channel. It featured scenes of *Dhamma Pajjota* and extracts of interviews with the conducting teacher, another assistant teacher and a student.

A large contingent of meditators from France had hired a bus to come to *Dhamma Pajjota* from Paris. Amongst them was a group of expatriate Cambodians, who had prepared sumptuous Cambodian food for the participants of the one-day course. This was supplemented by food prepared by meditators at *Dhamma Pajjota*. All of these loving efforts to prepare food were greatly appreciated!

During the lunch break Goenkaji devoted an hour for questions and answers with students. For most of the students on the course, it was their first chance to meet with Goenkaji and to meditate in his presence.

The one-day course came to a happy conclusion with the serving of tea and delicious pies, cooked in a nearby bakery by meditators. The weather had been pleasant all day, and even at this hour it remained warm and sunny. The meditators, though coming from so many different countries, seemed to have no difficulty communicating with each other. Many different languages could be heard as they conversed together happily. A large number of the visiting meditators stayed on at the center for the entire weekend.

Day 124, August 11, Dhamma Pajjota, Belgium

A European Union—Unity Amongst Meditators

Sunday was set aside for Goenkaji to meet with trusts and groups of meditators from different countries around Europe (and Israel). Both for countries with already established centers, and those just starting to organize courses, like Serbia and Scandinavia, it was a chance to discuss problems and responsibilities with Goenkaji. In the meetings, Goenkaji said that each country in Europe should have a legally recognized organization to manage courses, and at least one Vipassana center. He said that if the Vipassana trust in any country found that establishing a Vipassana center was beyond its financial or organizational means, it should work towards starting a Dhamma House as an interim step.

Goenkaji praised the unity shown by Vipassana meditators in Europe. *Dhamma Pajjota* in Belgium is a wonderful example of meditators transcending national and linguistic boundaries to come together for the purpose of Dhamma. When the center was bought, most of the seed money came from German meditators; now most of the Dhamma workers at the center are Dutch. As Goenkaji keeps saying—true spirituality always unites people. *Dhamma Pajjota* offers a shining example of this truth.

Students staying at *Dhamma Pajjota* volunteered to tackle many important jobs, such as erecting and taking down tents. Thanks to their service, the center management had been able to save significant amounts of *dāna* money, by hiring tents without the need for paid labor.

In the evening, Goenkaji gave an interview to a magazine columnist and also met with a number of teachers from different European countries. At about 10.30 p.m. he met with *Dhamma Pajjota's* building committee, which includes two architects, to review the proposed building plan for the center.

Day 125, August 12, Dhamma Pajjota, Belgium / Vught, Holland / Dhamma Pajjota, Belgium

Spirituality in Business, But Not Business in Spirituality

Goenkaji had been invited to be the keynote speaker at the "Spirit in Business" conference in Vught, Holland, organized as a European follow-up to a similar conference held earlier in New York. About 25 Vipassana meditators involved in business came from across Europe to attend the conference too. Most of the meditators who played an active part in the conference were young entrepreneurs.

Goenkaji spoke for about half an hour, and then answered questions for another 30 minutes or so. After his address, Goenkaji met with a journalist from a Dutch newspaper. In this discussion he emphasized the role of spirituality in business. As he often repeats, "There should be spirituality in business, but we should never make a business out of spirituality."

A decision was made to hold a special Vipassana course for business executives and leaders of society at *Dhamma Pajjota* in May 2003.

It was late in the evening when Goenkaji returned to *Dhamma Pajjota*.

Day 126, August 13, Dhamma Pajjota, Belgium / Cologne, Germany / Dhamma Pajjota, Belgium

Congress Hall, Cologne

In the morning, Goenkaji gave interviews to a Belgian newspaper, a leading financial newspaper, a Hindu newspaper and a Dutch political newspaper.

In the evening, he traveled to Germany by car to give a talk at the Congress Hall in Cologne. The venue was filled to capacity.

The caretaker informed the organizers that the 555-year old building was originally built as a marketplace, but after its completion came to be used as an assembly hall. About 500 years ago it was the scene of an emperor's coronation ceremony and served as the imperial court. Recently it was the venue for a meeting of the European Council. It is close to the Rhine River and within walking distance of the famous Cologne Domes.

In his talk, titled "Ethics and Mindfulness in Business," Goenkaji explained that Vipassana is mindfulness of the truth inside. The root cause of dishonesty, deceit and fraud in the corporate and business spheres is simple greed. Profiteering stems from greed, and greed stems from a lack of awareness of the truth inside.

Goenkaji was asked many questions at the end of the talk, answering as many as time permitted. He then moved to another room, where a press conference had been organized. Again, he was confronted with many questions. One journalist was keen to know why Goenkaji maintained a strict policy of not charging for Vipassana courses, even when doing so would provide him the financial resources to spread Vipassana further and wider. Goenkaji said that while the argument for charging might seem to be a good one on first consideration, any such venture was bound to harm Dhamma. If money were involved, sooner or later profit would become the most important motive of the enterprise, and course organizers would start making compromises to please their "customers." That is why the

Buddha warned so clearly against making a business out of Dhamma.

It was after midnight when Goenkaji returned to *Dhamma Pajjota*.

Day 127, August 14, Dhamma Pajjota, Dilsen, Belgium
Another Ten-Day Course Begins

Requests for media interviews with Goenkaji continued to pour in from around Belgium and neighboring countries, so Goenkaji made time for more interviews in the morning, including one with reporters from a financial daily and one with a German magazine for engineers.

In the evening, Goenkaji was interviewed by a television network that had come to report on his visit. The TV reporters were particularly interested to learn about the role of Vipassana in prison reforms. As it happened, two prison directors from Holland had arrived at the center to join the ten-day course that was just commencing.

In the afternoon, Goenkaji took a brief tour around the center. In the evening, he led the opening of the ten-day course, giving live Anapana instructions to the students. It was fitting that his last formal engagement of the tour was to lead the opening Anapana session of a ten-day course, because it is through such courses that people first learn Vipassana.

Over the past 33 years, Goenkaji has conducted hundreds of ten-day Vipassana courses in India and around the world. All this experience with hundreds of thousands of students has allowed him to perfect the structure of courses and graduated presentation of instructions and discourses. This course format has now been tested throughout the world, with people from a wide range of cultural, socioeconomic and religious backgrounds, proving highly effective in all situations. To train people in this universal technique taught by the Buddha, Goenkaji has applied essentially the same ten-day course format as used by his teacher and also his teacher's teacher, proving it to be an effective means of bringing the good restorative of Dhamma to suffering humanity everywhere.

Day 128, August 15, Dhamma Pajjota, Dilsen, Belgium
Meeting at European Union

On the last day of the European section of the "Meditation Now" tour 2002, Goenkaji met with the EU Commissioner for International Trade, Mr. Pascal Lamy. Goenkaji left the beautiful *Dhamma Pajjota* for the airport at 6.15 a.m. After checking in his luggage he made his way to the Headquarters to the European Union (EU) in Brussels. Being a public holiday, the streets and offices were deserted, but the security office at the EU were advised of Goenkaji's visit and so awaited him. A security officer escorted Goenkaji quickly to the Office of the Commissioner for Trade.

Mr. Lamy welcomed Goenkaji and thanked him for taking time to visit the EU. He congratulated Goenkaji on the success of his tour and expressed his pleasure at seeing this ancient method of mental culture (Vipassana) finding wider acceptance in the West. Mr. Lamy had already studied some of the literature he had been given earlier by a Vipassana meditator.

To a question from Mr. Lamy as to whether it is religious or non-religious people that are more attracted to Vipassana, Goenkaji answered, "Both." Religious people tend to find elements of their own religion in Vipassana, since morality, mastery over the mind and mental purity are common to all religions. On the other hand, non-religious people readily accept Vipassana too because of its scientific, practical nature.

Goenkaji then gave Mr. Lamy a basic outline of the technique of Vipassana. Goenkaji expressed his hope that society's leaders would accept Vipassana. By so doing they could bring enormous benefit to the people of today's troubled world.

Only 30 minutes had been set aside for the meeting, but Mr. Lamy asked Goenkaji if he could extend his stay. Since Goenkaji had already checked in his luggage at the airport he was able to remain a little longer. Next, Mr. Lamy asked Goenkaji about the socioeconomic and business conditions in India and in Myanmar (Burma). Goenkaji told him that he was no longer involved in politics or business, and that his entire focus was spirituality. Nonetheless, he praised Mr. Lamy's efforts to help the "Least Developed Countries," and his "Everything But Arms" initiative.

As the meeting concluded, Mr. Lamy commented that Goenkaji's approach of helping individuals to create a better society and the Western world's efforts to provide better material conditions for humanity were complementary. He wished peace and prosperity to the countries of India and Myanmar. In the end the meeting ran for some 60 minutes—twice the length originally planned.

Goenkaji was escorted to the gate of the building by the Chief of the Cabinet of Commissioner for Trade. He reached the airport in good time to catch his flight. Mataji was waiting there along with the meditators who had brought Goenkaji's party to the airport.

Chocolate Icing on the Dhamma Tour Cake

Just as if a person, overcome by hunger and exhaustion, were to receive a meal of honey cake, and wherever he bit into it would find it satisfying and delicious, to someone overcome by suffering, the Buddha's words are truthful, sweet, agreeable to the ear, salutary and auspicious.

Goenkaji is a committed practitioner and judicious master of the Buddha's teaching in all its richness and fullness. Nourished by his deep experiential wisdom, garnered over nearly half a century of devoted practice and more than three decades of lovingly teaching Dhamma to people all over the world, Goenkaji's Dhamma talks throughout this tour have been like a sweet cake. Everywhere he has gone, those who have listened to him have enjoyed the sweet, uplifting taste of Dhamma's benevolent nectar. All of his discourses during this long tour have inspired faith in Dhamma amongst those who previously had none, and enhanced the faith of those who were already inclined to Dhamma.

During Goenkaji's visit to Europe, the largest Vipassana course outside of South Asia was held—at the relatively new center of *Dhamma Pajjota* in Belgium. His public talks drew enthusiastic responses and the media showed so much interest in his message that Goenkaji found it difficult to satisfy the demand for interviews.

Belgium, a small country, famed for its chocolates, was the last stop on this remarkable four-month tour. It was the chocolate icing on the "Meditation Now" tour cake.

The Volunteers

The preparations for the 'Meditation Now' tour started many months before Goenkaji and Mataji left India.

The planning began in 2001 for the enormous logistical task of organizing programs all over the North American continent and ensuring the comfort of the elderly meditation masters as they moved across the country in a caravan of motor homes.

Detailed plans developed as students tried to anticipate all the needs of the tour. What was needed to look after Goenkaji, Mataji and a tour crew of about twenty? How could a system be created to provide prepared food and provisions across the whole of America for a caravan that had hardly any time to prepare food? What was necessary to prepare in advance to facilitate crossing the U.S.-Canada border four times in the middle of the tourist season with eight motor homes and twenty people from three countries? How could local communities be helped to prepare for the caravan, the day-sittings, the public talks, the local media events and business meetings?

The lists seemed endless and the task very difficult, but the enthusiastic and hardworking volunteers proved equal to it.

So many Vipassana meditators volunteered their time on the tour and gave valuable service. Here we give the list of only those who were actually on the caravan.

The names of the caravan crew do not appear in the diary.

Caravan Crew in North America

Most of the volunteers served only for some part of the tour.
(* Those who were on the caravan throughout the tour.)

    Elaichidevi Agarwal
    Eilona Ariel: Independent Support Crew
    Gail Beary : Independent Support Crew
    John Beary : Independent Support Crew
    Dhananjay Chavan* : Secretary to Principal Teacher
    Evie Chauncey : Independent Support Crew
    Jonathan Crowley* : Independent Film Crew
    David Crutcher : Maintenance, Driver
    Karen Donovan : Logistics Coordinator
    Tim Donovan : Driver
    Bill Hamilton : Independent Support Crew
    Virginia Hamilton : Independent Support Crew
    Lonnie Harris : Driver
    Lemay Henderson : Independent Support Crew
    Matt Iverson : Kitchen Assistant
    Larry Jack* : Recording Goenkaji's Talks
    Tim Lanning* : Caravan Technical Assistance, Driver
    Barry Lapping* : Coordinator, Vehicle Maintenance, Driver
    Kate Lapping* : Logistics Coordinator
    Bennett Miller* : Independent Film Crew
    Laura Mills : Caravan Food Coordinator
    Parker Mills : Vehicle Maintenance, Driver
    Patrick O'Neil* : Independent Book Distributor
    Lallie Pratt* : Independent Support Crew
    Ravi Kumar : Driver, Technical Assistance, Kitchen Assistant

Craig Rublee : Driver

Jeannine Rublee : Caravan Food Coordinator

Ruth Senturia* : Recording Goenkaji's Talks

Peter Simpson : Kitchen Assistant, Driver

Michael Stein : Assisting the Principal Teacher in New York and at Eastover

Bruce Stewart : Independent Support Crew

Maureen Stewart : Caravan Food Coordinator

Lily Thorne* : Independent Film Crew

Ben Turner* : Independent Book Distribution

Ram Pratap Yadav* : Assistant to Principal Teacher and Cook

The crew wishes to acknowledge the kind and selfless support of all the meditators who supported them along the way. In particular, the overall coordinators and all the local meditators at each stop who came forward to help with food, laundry, shopping, and local transportation in addition to organizing group sittings, one-day courses and Goenkaji's talks and media interviews. It is thanks to their help that the 'Meditation Now' tour was so successful.

List of Vipassana Meditation Centres

Offering ten-day residential Vipassana Meditation courses in the tradition of Sayagyi U Ba Khin, as taught by S. N. Goenka. (Non-centre courses are offered in many places throughout the world. For schedule of courses please contact Dhamma Giri or your nearest centre or visit www.vri.dhamma.org and www.dhamma.org)

India

Dhamma Giri & Dhamma Tapovana
Vipassana International Academy, Igatpuri, 422 403 Dist. Nashik, Maharashtra
Tel: [91] (02553) 244076, 244302, 244086; Fax: [91] (02553) 244176 email: <info@giri.dhamma.org> Web site: <www.vri.dhamma.org>

Dhamma Nāga, Nagpur, Tel: (0712) 2558686, 2527860; Fax: 2539716; e-mail: dhamma@nagpur.dot.net.in

Dhamma Sarovara, Dhule, Contact Tel: (02562) 222861, 224168, 229632, 202737. Email: dhammasarovara@indiatimes.com

Dhammānanda, Pune, Tel: (020) 24468903, 24464243
e-mail: webmaster@ananda.dhamma.org

Dhammālaya, Kolhapur, Tel: (0230) 2487167, Fax: 2487383. Email: dhammalaya@sancharnet.in

Dhamma Thalī, P.O. Box 208, Jaipur 302 001, Rajasthan, Tel: (0141) 2680220, 2680311; Fax: 2576283; e-mail: dhammjpr@datainfosys.

Dhamma Sota, Delhi, Tel: (011) 26452772. Mobile: 98110-45002; Fax: 26470658; e-mail: vipassana@dhammasota.org, Website: www.dhammasota.org

Dhamma Sikhara, Dharamashala, HP
Tel: (01892) 221309, 221368; e-mail: info@sikhara.dhamma.com

Dhamma Salila, Dehradun, UP Tel: (0135) 2754880, 2715189/27;
e-mail: assorep@nde.vsnl.net.in

Dhamma Dhaja, Hoshiarpur, Punjab. Tel: (01882) 272333, 240202;
Email: dhammadhaja@yahoo.com

Dhamma Tihār (Only for Prison Inmates), New Delhi.

Dhamma Cakka Sarnath, Tel: (0542) 2205418, Fax: 2202285,
Email: kambalghar@sancharnet.in

Dhamma Suvatthi, Jetavana Vipassana Meditation Centre, Katara Bypass, Sravasti-271845, Dist. Bahraich. Tel: (05252) 265439. Email: dhammasravasti@yahoo.com

Dhamma Sindhu, Kutch Vipassana Centre, Village-Bada, Tal. Mandvi, Dist. Kutch 370 475, Gujarat, Tel: (02834) 273612, 273304; e-mail: info@sindhu.dhamma.com

Dhamma Pīṭha, Ahmedabad, Tel: (079) 22171178, 25624631.
Fax: 2170561; e-mail: somtex@icenet.net

Dhamma Gaṅgā, Calcutta, Tel: [91] (033) 2553 2855. City Office: Tel: (033) 2242 3225 (R), 2471 0319. Fax: 22255174. Email: badani@vsnl.com

Dhamma Pāla, Bhopal, M.P. Contact Tel: Res. (0755) 2462351, 2468053; Fax: 2468197. e-mail: mpveneer@sancharnet.in

Dhamma Licchavī, Tel: (0621) 2240215, 2247760.
Email: puddagal@satyam.net.in
Dhamma Bodhi, Bodh Gaya, Tel: (0631) 2200 437
Dhamma Khetta, Vipassana International Meditation Centre, 12.6 km.
Nagarjunsagar Road, Kusumnagar, Vanasthali Puram,Hyderabad - 70, A P.
Tel: Off. (040) 2424 0290, City Off. 24241746:
Fax: C/o (040) 24240290; e-mail: vimc_hyd@hotmail.com
Dhamma Setu Chennai, Contact Tel: (044) 52011188, 52177200. Fax: 52011177. Email: dhammasetu@vsnl.net
Dhamma Paphulla, Bangalore, Contact Tel: (080) 22224330,
Fax: 22275776; e-mail: silksb@vsnl.com

Nepal
Dharmaśṛṅga, Nepal Vipassana Centre, Budhanilkanth, Muhan Pokhari, Kathmandu, Nepal. Tel: [977] (01) 4250581, 4225490; Fax: 4224 720, 4226 314; e-mail: nvc@htp.com.np
Dhamma Tarāi, Contact Tel: [977] (051) 522092, 580054; Fax: [977] (051) 580056, 522086, Email: jsmlfact@mail.com.np
Dhamma Jananī, Lumbini, Tel: [977] (071) 580282, 541549;
Email: info@janani.dhamma.org
Dhamma Birāṭa, Tel: Off. [977] (21)) 525486, Res. 527671; Fax: [977] (1) 526466; Email: info@birata.dhamma.org

Sri Lanka
Dhamma Kūṭa, Vipassana Meditation Centre, Mowbray, Hindagala, Peradeniya; Tel: [94] (070) 800 057; e-mail: dhamma@sltnet.lk
Dhamma Sobhā, Tel: [94] (25) 2221887.
Email: <dhammasobha@yahoo.com

Cambodia
Dhamma Kamboja
Cambodia Vipassana Centre, Next to Kompong Ko Buddhist Temple, P.O. Box 867, Dist. Koh Thom, Kandol Province, Phnom Penh 3, Cambodia.
Tel/Fax: C/o [855] (23) 210850;
e-mail: ivcc@forum.org.kh
Dhamma Aṅkura, Dhamma Laṭṭhikā

Indonesia
Dhamma Jāvā, Contact: Mrs Irene Wong,
Jl. Alam Asri VII, No. SK. 3, Pondok Indah, Jakarta Selatan 12310
Tel: & Fax: [62] (21) 765 4139, 750 2257; Email: info@java.dhamma.org

Japan
Dhamma Bhānu
Japan Vipassana Centre, Mizuho-Cho, Funai-Gun, Kyoto-Fu 62203, Japan.
Tel: [81] (0771) 860 765,
e-mail: info@bhanu.dhamma.org

Mongolia
Dhamma Maṅgala, C/o Mongolian Medical Centre, Ulaanbaater, Songino Hairhan Duureg, Mongolia 21/892, Tel: (976) 682636, 368064; Fax: [00] (976) 681176

Myanmar
Dhamma Joti, Vipassana Centre, Wingaba Yele Kyaung, Nga HtatGyi Pagoda Road, Bahan Township, Yangon, Myanmar Tel: [0095] (01) 546660 Office: Tel: [0095] (01) 253601, 245327, 281502, Fax: 248 174
e-mail: bandoola@mptmail.net.mm; goenka@ mptmail.net.mm
Dhamma Ratana, Mogok, Mobile: [95] (09) 6970840
Dhamma Maṇḍapa, Mandalay, Tel: [95] (02) 8023913, 6970173
Dhamma Makuta, Mogok, Mobile: [95] (09) 6970840
Dhamma Maṇḍala, Mandalay, Myanmar, Contact: Dhamma Joti

Taiwan
Dhammodaya, Tel: [886] (04) 581 4265, 582 3932;
Fax: [886] (04) 581 1503; e-mail: <tvc@tpts6.seed.net.tw>

Thailand
Dhamma Kamala, Thailand Vipassana Centre, 200 Baan Nerrnpasuk, Tambon Dongkeelek, Maung District, Prachinburi 25000, Thailand.
Tel/Fax: [66] (037) 403 515; Contact Tel: Res. [66] (02) 552 1731; Off. 521 0392. Fax: 552 1753
Dhamma Ābhā, Phitsanulok, Contact: Dhamma Kamala
Dhamma Suvaṇṇa, Bangkok, Tel : [66] (43) 242288, Fax : [66] (43) 364544;
e-mail : ittimonta@hotmail.com

Australia & New Zealand
Dhamma Bhūmi Tel: [61] (02) 4787 7436; Fax: [61] (02) 4787 7221
e-mail: info@bhumi.dhamma.org Website: www.bhumi.dhamma.org
Dhamma Rasmi Tel: [61] (07) 5485 2452; Fax: 5485 2907
e-mail: info@rasmi.dhamma.org Website: www.rasmi.dhamma.org
Dhamma Niketana, P. O. Box 10292 BC, Adelaide, SA 5000, Australia
Tel: [61] (08) 8278 8278; e-mail: info@sa.au.dhamma.org
Dhamma Padīpa, Vipassana Foundation of WA
4 Letitia Road, North Fremantle, Western Australia 6159, Australia
Tel: [61] (08) 9433 4858; Fax: [61] (08) 9433 4868
Dhamma Pabhā Tel: [61] (03) 6263 6785; e-mail:
info@pabha.dhamma.org Website: www.pabha.dhamma.org
Dhamma Āloka Tel: [61] (03) 5961 5722; Fax: [61] (03) 5961 5765
e-mail: info@aloka.dhamma.org Website: www.aloka.dhamma.org
Dhamma Medinī Burnside Road, RD3 Kaukapakapa, New Zealand
Tel: [64] (09) 420 5319

Europe
Dhamma Dīpa UK, Tel: [44] (01989) 730 234; Fax [44] (01989) 730 450
e-mail: info@dipa.dhamma.org
Dhamma Geha Germany, Tel: [49] (07083) 51169; Fax: 51328
e-mail: DhammaGeha@aol.com
Dhamma Dvāra
Vipassana Centre, Alte Str. 6, 08606 Triebel, Germany
Tel: [49] (37434) 79770; Fax: [49] (37434) 79771
e-mail: manager@dvara.dhamma.org

Dhamma Mahī France, Tel: [33] (0386) 457 514; Fax [33] (0386) 457 620
e-mail: info@mahi.dhamma.org
Dhamma Nilaya, Tel/Fax: [33] (1) 64751370; Mobile: 0609899079
e-mail: <vimuti@hotmail.com> and <aaksv@hotmail.com>
Dhamma Aṭala Italy, Tel/Fax [39] (0523) 857215;
e-mail: info@atala.dhamma.org
Dhamma Neru, Centro de Vipassana, Cami Can Ram, Els Bruguers, Apartado Postal 29, Santa Maria de Palautordero, 08460 Barcelona, Spain
Tel/Fax: [34] (93) 8482695; info@neru.dhamma.org
Dhamma Pajjota, Vipassana Belgium vzw, Driepaal 3, B - 3650 Dilsen-Stokkem, Belgium; Tel: [32] (08) 951 8230; Fax: [32] (08) 951 8239;
e-mail: vipassana.dilsen@skynet.be
Dhamma Sumeru, LaSalome, CH-2325, Les Planchettes, Switzerland
Tel: [41] (32) 9411670; Fax: 9411650 e-mail: info@sumeru.dhamma.org

North America

Dhamma Dharā Mass., Tel: [1] (413) 625 2160; Fax: [1] (413) 625 2170
e-mail: info@dhara.dhamma.org Website: www.dhara.dhamma.org
Dhamma Kuñja WA, Tel: [1] (360) 978 5434. Fax: [1] (360) 978 5433
e-mail: info@kunja.dhamma.org
Dhamma Mahāvana CA, Tel: [1] (559) 877 4386; Fax 877 4387
e-mail: info@mahavana.dhamma.org; website:
www.mahavana.dhamma.org
Dhamma Maṇḍa, Mendocino, CA, e-mail: info@manda.dhamma.org
Dhamma Sirī TX, Tel: [1] (972) 932 7868; Fax: 962-8858
Reg: (214) 521-5258, e-mail: info@siri.dhamma.org
Dhamma Surabhi B.C. V5Z 4R3, Canada. Tel: [1] (250) 3784506;
e-mail: info@surabhi.dhamma.org; Web-site: surbhi.dhamma.org
Dhamma Suttama, Quebec, Tel: [1] (514) 481 3504; Fax: 879 3437

Latin America

Dhamma Santi, Centro de Meditação Vipassana, Miguel Pereira, Brazil
Tel: [55](21) 2221-4985; Email: info@br.dhamma.org
Website: www.santi.dhamma.org

Publications of Vipassana Research Institute

English Publications

Sayagyi U Ba Khin Journal
Essence of Tipitaka by U Ko Lay
The Art of Living
The Discourse Summaries
Healing the Healer
    by Dr. Paul Fleischman
Come People of the World
Gotama the Buddha:
    His Life and His Teaching
The Gracious Flow of Dharma
Discourses on Satipatthana Sutta
The Wheel of Dhamma
    Rotates Around the World
Vipassana: Its Relevance
    to the Present World
Dharma: Its True Nature
Vipassana- Addiction & Health
    (Sminar 1989)
The Importance of Vedana
    and Sampajanya
Pagoda Souvenir 1997
Pagoda Seminar, Oct. 1997
A Re-appraisal of Patanjali's
    Yoga-Sutra by S. N. Tandon
The Manuals Of Dhamma
    by Ven. Ledi Sayadaw
Was the Buddha a Pessimist
Psychological Effects of Vipassana
    on Tihar Jail Inmates
Effect of Vipassana Meditation
    on Quality of Life (Tihar Jail)
For the Benefit of Many
Manual of Vipassana Meditation
Realising Change
The Clock of Vipassana Has Struck
Meditation Now - Inner Peace
    through Inner Wisdom
S. N. Goenka at the United Nation
Defence Against External Invasion
How to Defend the Republic
Why Was the Sakyan
    Republic Destroyed?
Mahasatipatthana Sutta
Pali Primer
Key to Pali Primer
Buddhagunagāthāvali (in three scripts)
Buddhasahassanāmāvali
    (in seven scripts)

हिन्दी, मराठी एवं अन्य प्रकाशन

निर्मल धारा धर्म की - (पांच दिवसीय प्रवचन)
प्रवचन सारांश (शिविर-प्रवचन)
जागे पावन प्रेरणा
जागे अंतर्बोध
धर्म: जीवन जीने की कला
तिपिटक में सम्यक संबुद्ध, भाग-१, २
धारण करे तो धर्म
क्या बुद्ध दुःखवादी थे?
मंगल जगे गृही जीवन में
धम्मवाणी संग्रह (पालि गाथाएं एवं हिंदी अनु.)
विपश्यना पगोडा स्मारिका
सुत्तसार भाग १ (दीघ एवं मज्झिम निकाय)
सुत्तसार भाग २ (संयुत्तनिकाय)
सुत्तसार भाग ३ (अंगुत्तर एवं खुद्दकनिकाय)
धन्य बाबा!
कल्याणमित्र सत्यनारायण गोयन्का (व्यक्तित्व और कृतित्व)
पातंजल योगसूत्र
आहुनेय्य, पाहुनेय्य, अंजलिकरणीय डॉ. ओम प्रकाश जी
राजधर्म [कुछ ऐतिहासिक प्रसंग]
आत्म-कथन भाग-१
लोक गुरु बुद्ध
देश की बाह्य सुरक्षा
गणराज्य की सुरक्षा कैसे हो!
शाक्यों और कोलियों के गणतंत्र का विनाश क्यों हुआ?
अंगुत्तर निकाय, भाग-१
मंगल हुआ प्रभात (हिंदी दोहे)
जागो लोगां जगत रा (राजस्थानी दूहा)
धम्मगीत (पालि गाथाएं, हिंदी अनुवाद)
धम्मपद (संशोधित हिंदी अनुवाद सहित)
महासतिपट्ठानसुत्त (समीक्षा सहित भाषानुवाद)
बुद्धगुणगाथावली (पालि)
बुद्धसहस्सनामावली (पालि)
शांतिपथ (मराठी)
जागे पावन प्रेरणा (मराठी)
प्रवचन सारांश (मराठी)
धर्म: जीवन जगण्याची कला (मराठी)
जागे अंतर्बोध (मराठी)
प्रवचन सारांश (गुजराती)
धर्म: जीवन जीववानी कला (गुजराती)
महासतिपट्ठानसुत्त (गुजराती अनुवाद सहित)
जागे अंतर्बोध (गुजराती)
धारण करे तो धर्म (गुजराती)
जागे पावन प्रेरणा
क्या बुद्ध दुःख वादी थे?
विपश्यना शा माटे? (गुजराती पुस्तिका)
होश का सफ़र (उर्दू)
द आर्ट ऑफ लिविंग (तमिल)

Pāli Literature

Pāli Tipiṭaka with its commentarial literature in Devanāgarī script
Buddhasahassanāmāvalī (Pāli verses by Goenkaji) (in Roman, Devanāgarī, Myanmar, Sinhalese, Thai, Cambodian, and Mongolian scripts) and
Buddhaguṇagāthāvalī (Pāli verses by Goenkaji) (in Roman, Devanāgarī and Myanmar scripts)
Chaṭṭha Saṅgāyana CD-ROM containing Pāli literature in seven scripts
For more information write to: **Vipassana Research Institute**, Dhamma Giri, Igatpuri 422 403, India. Tel: [91] (02553) 244076, 244086; Fax: 244176
e-mail: info@giri.dhamma.org   website: www.vri.dhamma.org